D1537247

Café & Restaurant Design

teNeues

Imprint

Produced by fusion publishing GmbH, Berlin   www.fusion-publishing.com

Editorial team:

Mariel Marohn, Manuela Roth (Editors)

Bianca Maria Öller (Text)

Kerstin Klose, Manuela Roth (Layout), Jan Hausberg, Janine Minkner (Imaging & Pre-press)

Connexus GmbH, Sprachentransfer, Berlin (Translations)

Cover photo (location): Frank Tjepkema (Praq Restaurant)

Back cover photos from top to bottom (location): Dianna Snape (Gingerboy), courtesy Hayonstudio / Nienke Klunder (La Terraza del Casino), Jürgen Eheim (Acquadulza), CI&A Photography (Nooch Express), courtesy Adlon Holding GmbH (MĀ Restaurant)

Introduction photos (page, location): Pierluigi Piu (page 3, Olivomare), courtesy Au Quai Restaurant / Gulliver Theis (page 4, Au Quai Restaurant), Eric Axene (page 5, Blue Velvet Restaurant), Frank Tielemans (page 6, Eetbar Dit), Dimitrios Tsigos (page 7, Frame Bar), Frank Tjepkema (page 8, Praq Restaurant), Dianna Snape (page 9, Gingerboy), Joseph Burns (page 10, Wahaca), Åke Eson Lindman (page 11, Kungsholmen), Joachim Frydman (page 12, Le Saut du Loup), Riccardo Cordera (page 13, Grill-X), courtesy Hayonstudio / Nienke Klunder (page 14, La Terraza del Casino), courtesy Negro de Anglona / Luis Hevia (page 15, Negro de Anglona)

Published by teNeues Publishing Group

teNeues Verlag Gmbh + Co. KG
Am Selder 37
47906 Kempen, Germany
Tel.: 0049-(0)2152-916-0
Fax: 0049-(0)2152-916-111
E-mail: books@teneues.de

teNeues Publishing Company
16 West 22nd Street
New York, NY 10010, USA
Tel.: 001-212-627-9090
Fax: 001-212-627-9511

teNeues Publishing UK Ltd.
York Villa, York Road
Byfleet
KT14 7HX, Great Britain
Tel.: 0044-1932-403509
Fax: 0044-1932-403514

teNeues France S.A.R.L.
93, rue Bannier
45000 Orléans, France
Tel.: 0033-2-38541071
Fax: 0033-2-38625340

Press department: arehn@teneues.de
Tel.: 0049-2152-916-202

www.teneues.com

ISBN: 978-3-8327-9323-4

© 2009 teNeues Verlag GmbH + Co. KG, Kempen

Printed in Italy

Bibliographic information published by the Deutsche Nationalbibliothek.
The Deutsche Nationalbibliothek lists this publication in the Deutsche Nationalbibliografie;
detailed bibliographic data are available in the Internet at http://dnb.d-nb.de.

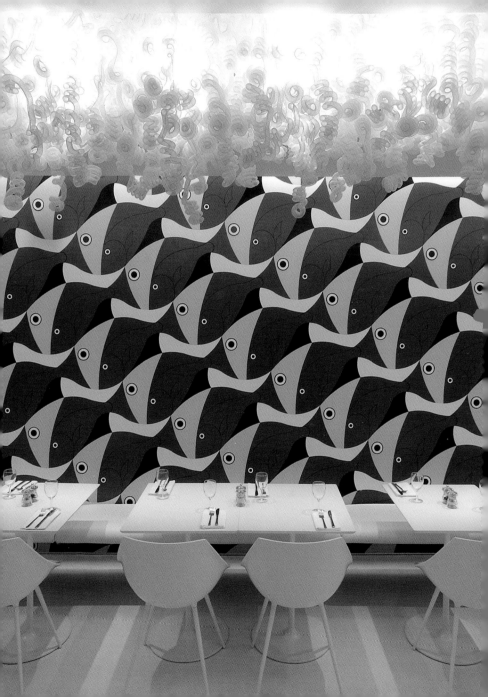

EUROPE

AMERICAS

ASIA/AUSTRALIA

Introduction

Cafés and restaurants are places where people come together to exchange their thoughts and stories—places full of creativity and inspiration. Good taste is in authority here with excited conversations, culinary delights and exquisite drinks.

This is reflected in today's keen to experiment design: creative architects show all over the world, how diversified and innovative, but sometimes also traditional and modern the ambience around food and communication can be. Part of this are interesting room concepts that open new dimensions such as wall and window designs which let the eye sweep, or daring material or style mixtures which abandon all seen before and set new trends. And last but not least surprising furniture designs that are inspiring and invite guests to feel good.

This book presents 39 international cafés and restaurants which prove that gastronomy can be something special, really unique and thus open new ways of interior design. Accountable for the design and development are both so far unknown newcomers and established star designers and architects such as Philippe Starck or Kengo Kuma. On the following pages you are invited to discover the hottest spots in cosmopolitan cities such as New York, Mumbai and Rio de Janeiro. Plus real insider tips such as Innsbruck or Maccagno.

Bianca Maria Öller

Einleitung

Cafés und Restaurants sind Orte, an denen Menschen zusammenkommen, um sich auszutauschen. Orte voller Kreativität und Inspiration. Hier hat der gute Geschmack das Sagen – bei angeregter Unterhaltung, kulinarischen Genüssen und köstlichen Getränken.

Dies findet in dem heutigen, von Experimentierfreude geprägten Design seine Entsprechung: Kreative Architekten zeigen auf der ganzen Welt, wie abwechslungsreich und innovativ, manchmal aber auch traditionell und zugleich doch modern das Ambiente rund ums Speisen und Kommunizieren sein kann. Dazu gehören interessante Raumkonzepte, die neue Dimensionen eröffnen, wie etwa Wand- und Fenstergestaltungen, die das Auge schweifen lassen, oder wagemutige Material- oder Stilmixturen, die alles bisher Dagewesene über Bord werfen und neue Trends setzen. Und nicht zuletzt überraschende Möbelentwürfe, die inspirieren und zum Wohlfühlen einladen.

Dieses Buch stellt 39 internationale Cafés und Restaurants vor, die beweisen, dass Gastronomie etwas Besonderes, wirklich Einmaliges sein kann und so neue Wege des Interieur Designs eröffnen. Verantwortlich dafür zeichnen sowohl noch unbekannte Newcomer als auch etablierte Stardesigner und -architekten wie Philippe Starck oder Kengo Kuma. Entdecken Sie auf den folgenden Seiten die angesagtesten Spots in Weltstädten wie New York, Mumbai und Rio de Janeiro. Und echte Geheimtipps, zum Beispiel in Innsbruck oder Maccagno.

Bianca Maria Öller

Introduction

Les cafés et les restaurants sont des lieux de rencontre et d'échange, des lieux qui favorisent la créativité et l'inspiration. C'est là que le bon goût fait valoir ses droits – que ce soit par des conversations animées, des délices culinaires ou de délicieuses boissons.

C'est aussi ce que reflète le design actuel épris du besoin d'expérimenter : dans le monde entier des architectes créatifs montrent comment l'ambiance des restaurants, lieux de la communication et de la convivialité, peut se métamorphoser en recourrant à la variété et aux innovations mais aussi à une tradition revivifiée par une interprétation moderne. Cette tendance s'affirme par des conceptions de l'espace fascinantes qui créent de nouvelles dimensions : la forme des fenêtres ou des décorations murales captivent et entraînent le regard. Des associations de matériaux audacieuses ou des mélanges de styles inédits rompent avec les conventions qui ont prévalu jusqu'à ce jour pour déboucher sur de nouveaux horizons. Le mobilier soutient aussi ces nouvelles tendances : des conceptions surprenantes ouvrent de nouvelles voies à l'imagination et à l'inspiration sans négliger le bien-être.

Ce livre présente quelques 39 cafés et restaurants internationaux : ils montrent que la gastronomie peut devenir une expérience particulière, vraiment unique et ouvrir ainsi de nouvelles voies au design intérieur. Ce mouvement est porté aussi bien par de nouveaux venus encore inconnus que par des designers et architectes de premier plan bien établis tels que Philippe Starck ou Kengo Kuma. Découvrez, dans les pages qui suivent, les endroits les plus en vogue dans les grandes villes du monde telles que New York, Mumbai et Rio de Janeiro. Mais aussi de vrais secrets qui vous attendent à Innsbruck ou Maccagno, par exemple.

Bianca Maria Öller

Introducción

Cafés, restaurantes, bares y similares son todos ellos lugares donde las personas se reúnen para intercambiar ideas, lo que les convierte en sitios llenos de creatividad e inspiración. Son lugares donde domina el buen gusto, en medio y rodeado de conversaciones animadas, delicias culinarias y bebidas tentadoras.

Este ambiente encuentra su correspondencia en los diseños que dominan la actualidad y que tanto se caracterizan por el placer del experimento: en todo el mundo los arquitectos y diseñadores más creativos se esfuerzan en demostrar lo cambiante e innovador, a veces con un toque tradicional aunque no obstante moderno, en que se pueden realizar los ambientes que rodean la buena mesa y la comunicación. Esta idea incluye conceptos ambientales interesantes que abren nuevas dimensiones, como lo son las paredes y ventanas que invitan a dar un paseo visual, así como sus osadas combinaciones de estilo y material que se desentienden de todo lo anterior y marcan tendencias nuevas. Y no en último lugar, sorprendentes diseños de muebles que inspiran e invitan al confort.

Este libro presenta 39 cafés y restaurantes internacionales que demuestran que la gastronomía puede ser algo especial y realmente único y, de esta manera, abre nuevos caminos para el diseño de interiores. Los responsables de estas obras son algunos Newcomers aún sin conocer al igual que diseñadores y arquitectos estándar ya conocidos como Philippe Starck o Kengo Kuma. Descubra en las páginas que siguen a continuación los lugares más In en las capitales del mundo como Nueva York, Mumbai o Río de Janeiro y, además, algunos rincones todavía por descubrir, por ejemplo en Innsbruck o en Maccagno.

Bianca Maria Öller

Introduzione

Caffè e ristoranti sono luoghi nei quali gli uomini si incontrano e conversano. Luoghi densi di creatività e di ispirazione. E' questo il luogo dove il buon gusto dice la sua – in presenza di un vivace intrattenimento, di godimenti culinari e di bibite squisite.

Tutto questo trova la sua corrispondenza nel design odierno caratterizzato dal piacere di sperimentare: Architetti creativi mostrano in tutto il mondo quanto l'ambiente collegato al mangiare e al comunicare possa essere vario ed innovativo, o talvolta anche tradizionale e allo stesso tempo moderno. A questo ambito appartengono interessanti concetti spaziali che si aprono a nuove dimensioni, quali ad esempio allestimenti di pareti e di finestre che permettono all'occhio di vagare, oppure temerarie mescolanze di materiali e di stili, che gettano a mare tutto ciò che è esistito fino ad ora e stabiliscono nuovi trend. Vi sono anche abbozzi di mobilio sorprendenti, i quali sono fonte di ispirazione e invitano al benessere.

Questo libro presenta 39 caffè e ristoranti internazionali, i quali provano come la gastronomia possa essere qualcosa di speciale e di veramente unico, e in questo modo aprono nuove strade del design per interni. Guidano questo trend sia progettisti ed architetti ancora sconosciuti che professionisti già affermati quali Philippe Starck o Kengo Kuma. Scoprite nelle pagine seguenti i locali più alla moda in città mondiali quali New York, Mumbai e Rio de Janeiro. Vi sono anche consigli confidenziali, come ad esempio ad Innsbruck e a Maccagno.

Bianca Maria Öller

EUROPE

Kungsholmen

Stockholm I Sweden

www.kungsholmen.com
Architecture: Thomas Sandell
www.sandellsandberg.se
Photos: Åke Eson Lindman

200 guests can be seated in this large restaurant at Lake Mälaren in Stockholm. What sounds like a big canteen, however, is a fancy restaurant that, in fact, offers something for every taste with its seven different cuisines. Simple furniture, a modern open concept and the striking yellow shades make Kungsholmen a special food venue—where VIPs regularly make their appearance.

In dem großen Restaurant am Mälaren See in Stockholm haben 200 Gäste Platz. Doch was sich nach einer großen Kantine anhört, ist tatsächlich ein originelles Restaurant, das mit sieben verschiedenen Küchen jeden Geschmack trifft. Schlichte Möbel, ein modernes, offenes Konzept und die markanten gelben Lampenschirme machen das Kungsholmen zu einem besonderen Schauplatz des Essens – an dem sich regelmäßig auch Stars einfinden.

Ce restaurant spacieux au bord du lac Mälaren à Stockholm peut accueillir quelques 200 personnes. Or, ce local, qui par ses seules dimensions risquerait d'évoquer une grande cantine, réussit à s'imposer comme un restaurant original capable de satisfaire à tous les goûts en recourant à sept types de cuisines différents ! Des meubles simples, une conception moderne et ouverte de l'espace et des luminaires aux abat-jour d'un jaune caractéristique font du Kungsholmen un théâtre particulier de l'évènement culinaire – où des vedettes des médias ne manquent pas se montrer régulièrement.

En el espacioso restaurante en la orillas del lago de Mälaren en Estocolmo se dispone de sitio para 200 comensales. No obstante, lo que a primera vista nos suena como una cantina de una gran empresa en realidad es un restaurante realmente original el cual, gracias a sus siete cocinas distintas, es capaz de satisfacer a todos los gustos. El mobiliario que destaca por su simpleza, el concepto moderno totalmente abierto y las vistosas pantallas de las lámparas en amarillo chillón convierten al Kungsholmen en una especie de evento culinario del que también participan con asiduidad las celebridades.

Nel grande ristorante posto sul lago di Mälaren a Stoccolma vi è posto per 200 persone. Ciò che apparterrebbe ad una grande mensa, rappresenta invece una caratteristica di un ristorante originale, che accontenta ogni gusto con sette diversi tipi di cucina. Mobili sobri, un'impostazione moderna e aperta, nonché paralumi gialli pronunciati, rendono il Kungsholmen un luogo del mangiare per antonomasia – frequentato regolarmente anche da star.

Mathias Dahlgren

Stockholm I Sweden

www.mathiasdahlgren.com
Architecture: Studioilse (Creative direction & design)
www.studioilse.com
Photos: Lisa Cohen

Mathias Dahlgren's food philosophy of creating the new Swedish identity, being proud of it's herit-age whilst open to new experiences, was the starting point. Studioilse's design expresses this new concept, physically and emotionally, sensorially and subliminally. The Matsalen (dining room) and the Matbaren (food bar) are two spaces that can be smelt, heard and felt in very different ways.

Der Beginn war Mathias Dahlgrens Speisenphilosophie, die neue schwedische Identität zu kreieren. Dabei war er stolz auf sein kulturelles Erbe, gleichzeitig aber auch offen für neue Erfahrungen. Das Design von Studioilse drückt dieses neue Konzept aus – physisch und emotional, sensorisch und unterschwellig. Matsalen (Esszimmer) und Matbaren (Food Bar) sind zwei Räume, die auf viele unterschiedliche Arten gerochen, gehört und gefühlt werden können.

La philosophie des aliments de Mathias Dahlgren, qui se veut de créer la nouvelle identité suédoise, fière de son héritage tout en étant ouverte à de nouvelles expériences, a été le point de départ. Le design de Studioilse exprime ce nouveau concept, physiquement et émotionnellement, sensuellement et souverainement. Le matsalen (la salle à manger) et le matbaren (le bar-restaurant) sont deux espaces où tous les sens sont à la fête.

El punto de partida fue la filosofía culinaria de Mathias Dahlgren enfocada a la creación de la nueva identidad sueca, orgullosa de su herencia y al mismo tiempo abierta a nuevas experiencias. El diseño de Studioilse expresa este nuevo concepto, tanto desde el punto de vista físico y emocional como sensorial y subliminal. El Matsalen (comedor) y el Matbaren (bar) son dos espacios que se pueden oler, oír y sentir de multitud de maneras.

La filosofia alimentare di Mathias Dahlgren, tesa a creare la nuova identità svedese, fiera della propria eredità culturale pur con aperture a nuove esperienze, ha rappresentato il punto di partenza. Il design creato dallo Studioilse esprime questo nuovo concetto da in modo fisico, emozionale, sensoriale e subliminale. Il Matsalen (sala da pranzo) ed il Matbaren (food bar) rappresentano due spazi che possono essere annusati, sentiti e percepiti in modi diversi.

Eetbar Dit

Den Bosch I Netherlands

www.eetbar-dit.nl
Architecture: Studio Boot
www.studioboot.nl
Photos: Frank Tielemans

The Dutch design studio Studio Boot got the order to create a restaurant, where both parents and children feel home immediately. The Eetbar Dit is the result of this. Patterned tiles, colorful painted furniture and an open kitchen make guests of this restaurant feel as if they were sitting at home in their friends' kitchen. By the way, the bold furniture has been created by both established and young, so far unknown, designers.

Das holländische Designstudio Studio Boot bekam den Auftrag, ein Restaurant zu kreieren, in dem sich Erwachsene und Kinder auf Anhieb zu Hause fühlen. Herausgekommen ist dabei die Eetbar Dit. Gemusterte Fliesen, farbig lackierte Möbel und eine offene Küche geben den Gästen das Gefühl, bei Freunden zu Hause in der Küche zu sitzen. Das freche Mobiliar kommt dabei übrigens von etablierten ebenso wie von jungen, unbekannten Designern.

Le studio de design hollandais, Studio Boot a reçu l'ordre de concevoir un restaurant où, d'emblée, les adultes et les enfants puissent se sentir à l'aise. C'est ainsi que le Eetbar Dit a été créé. Des carrelages rehaussés de différents motifs, des meubles peints et une cuisine ouverte donnent aux visiteurs l'impression d'être dans une cuisine, chez des amis. Le mobilier enjoué a été conçu, par ailleurs, aussi bien par des designers à la réputation bien établie que par de jeunes designers encore inconnus.

El estudio de diseñadores Studio Boot en Holanda en Holanda recibió el encargo de crear un restaurante en el que se lograba que tanto los mayores como los niños que se encontrasen en casa nada más entrar. El resultado de este encargo es el actual restaurante Eetbar Dit. Los típicos alicatados holandeses de distinto color y diseño, los muebles rústicos de madera pintada y la cocina abierta, todo ello transmite la sensación de estar sentado en la cocina de unos amigos. Por cierto, el mobiliario fresco y atrevido es la obra de diseñadores ya establecidos y otros jóvenes desconocidos.

Lo studio di progettazione olandese Studio Boot è stato incaricato di creare gli interni di un ristorante, nel quale adulti e bambini si sentano subito come a casa propria. Il risultato è stato l'Eetbar Dit. Piastrelle a disegni, mobili laccati a colori ed una cucina aperta danno agli ospiti la sensazione di trovarsi nella cucina della casa di amici. L'irriverente mobilio è stato progettato da professionisti affermati ma anche da progettisti giovani e sconosciuti.

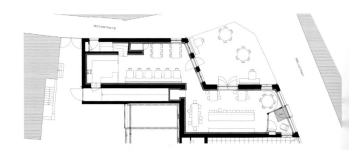

Praq Restaurant

Amersfoort I Netherlands

www.praq.nl
Architecture: Tjep.
www.tjep.com
Photos: Frank Tjepkema

The concept of the restaurant in Amersfoort was to create a frisky place, where both parents and children are comfortable. It almost goes without saying here, that one of the tables is shaped like a toy bus—or like a car. In combination with many puristic white elements and linear forms, a restaurant came into existence, which is as elegant as familial and child-friendly.

Die Idee des Restaurants in Amersfoort war, einen verspielten Ort zu schaffen, an dem sich Eltern wie Kinder gleichermaßen wohlfühlen. Hier ist es fast selbstverständlich, dass einer der Tische die Form eines Spielzeugbusses hat. Oder die eines Autos. Kombiniert mit vielen puristisch weißen Elementen und linearen Formen, entstand so ein Restaurant, das ebenso elegant wie familiär und kinderfreundlich ist.

L'idée directrice de ce restaurant à Amersfoort était de créer un lieu ludique où les parents tout aussi bien que les enfants puissent se sentir à l'aise. Dans ce local, il va presque de soi que quelques-unes des tables aient la forme de jouets : celle d'un bus ou d'une voiture. Ce mobilier, combiné à beaucoup d'éléments blancs, puristes et de formes linaires concourt à créer un restaurant ouvert aux enfants aussi élégant que familier.

La idea detrás de este restaurante de Amersfoort fue el crear un lugar lúdico que proporcionara el mismo placer de bienestar tanto a los padres como a los niños. Así no sorprende y se considera casi normal que una de las mesas tenga la forma de un autobús de juguete y otra la de un coche, ¿porqué no? Combinados estos diseños con elementos blancos puristas y formas lineales, se ha creado un restaurante que resulta tan elegante como a la vez familiar y apto para niños.

L'idea del ristorante di Amersfoort era quella di creare un luogo di svago nel quale sia i genitori che i figli si sentissero a proprio agio. E' quasi normale che in luogo come questo uno dei tavoli abbia la forma di autobus giocattolo. Oppure di un'automobile. Combinato con molti elementi puristici di colore bianco e forme lineari, è nato un ristorante che è allo stesso tempo elegante e adatto ai bambini.

Olivomare

London I UK

www.olivolondon.com
Architecture: Pierluigi Piu
www.pierluigipiu.it
Photos: Pierluigi Piu

The Olivomare in London exclusively committed itself to seafood—and also transferred this concept to the interior. The wall design therefore reminds guests of shoals and gentle swell. An innovative light concept creates diffuse light beams, which is suggestive of refracted sunlight under water. The sober white tables and chairs stylishly follow this impression by staying in the background at the same time.

Das Olivomare in London hat sich ausschließlich dem Seafood verschrieben – und dieses Konzept auch auf das Interieur übertragen. So erinnert die Wandgestaltung an Fischschwärme und sanften Wellengang. Ein innovatives Beleuchtungskonzept erzeugt diffuse Lichtstrahlen, was den Eindruck gebrochenen Sonnenlichts unter Wasser erweckt. Gleichzeitig halten sich die nüchternen, weißen Tische und Stühle stilvoll zurück.

Le restaurant Olivomare à Londres s'est voué exclusivement au poisson – et cette conception a été étendue à l'aménagement intérieur. C'est ainsi que la décoration des murs évoque des bancs de poissons et une douce houle. La conception innovante de l'éclairage recourt à des luminaires dont les rayons diffus créent l'illusion d'une lumière solaire sous-marine, infiniment réfractée. Parallèlement, les tables et les chaises blanches, sobres et de bon goût, soutiennent cette impression en restant à l'arrière-plan.

El restaurante Olivomare de Londres se dedica exclusivamente al Seafood... y también ha transferido este concepto al interiorismo. De ahí que todo el concepto de las paredes revoca el movimiento de los bancos de peces y el suave vaivén de las olas. Otro concepto innovador, el de la iluminación, crea rayos de luz difusos que transmiten la sensación del buceador observando los rayos del sol traspasando la superficie del agua. Para no intervenir en este ambiente ni mucho menos disturbarlo, las mesas y sillas blancas en extremo sobrias, de manera concienzuda y buscando se mantienen en segundo plano.

Il ristorante Olivomare di Londra è esclusivamente dedicato al cibo marino, ed al mondo del mare sono ispirati anche i suoi interni. Il trattamento delle pareti evoca banchi di pesci vaganti ed un dolce moto di onde, mentre l'innovativa concezione dell'illuminazione genera bagliori di luce diffusa e l'impressione di raggi solari spezzati sott'acqua. Le sedie e i tavoli bianchi, estremamente sobri, restano discretamente in secondo piano per non interferire con la caratterizzazione dell'ambiente.

Sake No Hana

London I UK

www.sakenohana.com
Architecture: Kengo Kuma
www.kkaa.co.jp
Photos: Junkichi Tatsuki

A piece of Japan right in the center of London—with the Sake No Hana, architect Kengo Kuma and gastronome Alan Yau created a restaurant that, at large, airs Japanese flair. And all this completely without any decoration knick-knack. Window fronts of more than four meters, a playfully light ceiling construction made of wood beams and black paint surfaces create the perfect ambience for the treat of Japanese sake on the typical Tatami mats.

Ein Stück Japan mitten in London – Architekt Kengo Kuma und Gastronom Alan Yau haben mit dem Sake No Hana ein Restaurant geschaffen, das in seiner Gesamtheit japanisches Flair ausstrahlt. Und dies ganz ohne Dekorations-Schnickschnack. Über vier Meter hohe Fensterfronten, eine spielerisch leichte Deckenkonstruktion aus Holzbalken und schwarze Lackflächen erzeugen hier das perfekte Ambiente für den Genuss japanischen Sakes auf den typischen Tatamimatten.

Le Japon au centre de Londres – l'architecte Kengo Kuma et le restaurateur Alan Yau ont créé un restaurant, le Sake No Hana qui, par l'ensemble qu'il constitue, reflète une ambiance japonaise. Et ceci sans devoir du tout recourir aux mièvreries de la décoration. Les fenêtres de plus de quatre mètres de haut et un plafond d'une légèreté enjouée constitué par des poutres de bois et des surfaces laquées noires créent ici une ambiance parfaite pour la dégustation de Sakes japonais sur des nattes caractéristiques de Tatami.

Un trozo de Japón en pleno Londres – con el restaurante Sake No Hana el arquitecto Kengo Kuma, junto con el gastrónomo Alan Yau, han creado un lugar que en su conjunto muy logrado ha sabido transmitir el aire japonés auténtico… y todo sin las típicas tonterías decorativas. Frontales de ventana de más de cuatro metros de altura, una estructura de techo juguetona y ligera de vigas de madera que alternan con superficies lacadas negras, crean el ambiente perfecto y original para saborear el saque japonés y sentarse en los tatamis típicos que se encuentran por doquier.

Un pezzo di Giappone nel bel mezzo di Londra – con il Sake No Hana l'architetto Kengo Kuma ed il gastronomo Alan Yau hanno creato un ristorante che nella sua totalità irradia un'atmosfera giapponese. E tutto questo senza cianfrusaglie decorative. Finestre alte oltre quattro metri, una struttura del soffitto scherzosamente leggera fatta di travi in legno e di superfici verniciate di colore nero generano in questo luogo il perfetto ambiente per gustare Sake giapponesi sui tipici tatami.

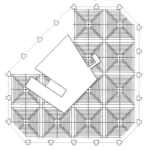

Wahaca

London I UK

www.wahaca.co.uk
Architecture: Softroom
www.softroom.com
Photos: Joseph Burns

Wahaca Restaurant, in London, has been inspired by the Mexican street markets. The cuisine's freshness and sophistication contrasts with the simple rustic presentation, matched in the corresponding furniture and design: reclaimed wood, shot blasted concrete, leather and original Mexican decorations fill this restaurant with Latin-American spirit. Illuminated surfaces in bright shades of green, blue and yellow thereby underline the fresh and simple character of Wahaca.

Die Straßenmärkte von Mexiko waren die Inspiration für das Restaurant Wahaca in London. Die Frische und Natürlichkeit der Küche finden sich auch im entsprechenden Design wieder: viel Holz, Leder und original mexikanische Dekorationen bringen lateinamerikanischen Spirit ins Lokal. Illuminierte Flächen in fröhlichen Grün-, Blau- und Gelbtönen unterstreichen dabei den frischen und einfachen Charakter des Wahaca.

Les marchés de rue de Mexico ont fourni l'inspiration du restaurant Wahaca à Londres. La fraîcheur et le naturel de la cuisine se retrouvent aussi dans le design correspondant : beaucoup de bois, de cuir et des décorations mexicaines originales font vivre l'esprit sud américain dans le local. Des surfaces illuminées dans des couleurs joyeuses vertes, bleus et jaunes souligne la fraîcheur et la simplicité caractéristique du Wahaca.

La inspiración para el restaurante Wahaca en Londres proviene de los mercadillos mejicanos en plena calle. El frescor y la naturalidad de la cocina se encuentran correspondidos en el diseño: mucha madera, cuero y decoración original mejicana se encargan de aportar al local el espíritu latino americano. Las superficies iluminadas con alegres tonalidades de verde, azul y amarillo subrayan nada más el carácter fresco y simple del Wahaca.

I mercati di strada del Messico hanno rappresentato l'ispirazione per il ristorante Wahaca di Londra. Freschezza e naturalezza della cucina si ritrovano anche nell'impostazione degli interni del ristorante: molto legno, cuoio e decorazioni originali messicane portano uno spirito latino-americano nel locale. Superfici illuminate in gioiose tonalità di verde, blu e giallo mettono l'accento sul carattere fresco e simpatico del Wahaca.

Baccarat

Paris I France

www.baccarat.fr
Architecture: Philippe Starck
www. philippe-starck.com
Photos: Claude Weber (pages 49–51), Roland Bauer (pages 52–55)

Maison Baccarat, the flagship store of the famous crystal producer, also houses the in-house restaurant apart from a shop and a museum. Since Philippe Starck re-designed it, this restaurant perfectly combines tradition and modernity: crystal chandeliers in fish tanks, a lot of glass and silver as well as straight, modern pieces of furniture await guests in the manor-house from 1884.

Im Maison Baccarat, dem Flagship-Store des berühmten Kristallproduzenten, befindet sich neben einem Shop und einem Museum auch das hauseigene Restaurant. Dieses bietet seit dem Redesign durch Philippe Starck die perfekte Verbindung von Tradition und Moderne: In dem Herrenhaus aus dem Jahr 1884 erwarten kristallene Lüster in Aquarien, viel Glas und Silber sowie geradlinige, moderne Möbelstücke die Gäste.

Le restaurant de la Maison Baccarat, le magasin phare du célèbre producteur de cristal, se trouve à proximité d'un magasin et d'un musée. Depuis que celui-ci a été remodelé par le designer Philippe Starck il offre une transition parfaite entre la tradition et la modernité : dans cet hôtel particulier, datant de 1884, des lustres de cristal, placés dans des aquariums, une multitude d'objets en verre et en argent, voisinent avec des meubles modernes aux lignes claires.

En la Maison Baccarat, la tienda bandera del famoso fabricante de objetos de cristal, también se encuentra, flanqueado por una tienda y un museo, el restaurante de la casa. Desde su rediseño por Philippe Starck representa la unión perfecta entre la tradición y lo moderno: en la residencia señorial, un edificio construido en el año 1884, lo que espera a los comensales son arañas de cristal en acuarios y mucho cristal y plata en combinación con muebles muy modernos de líneas completamente rectas.

Nella Maison Baccarat, il negozio portabandiera del noto produttore di cristalli, si trova, oltre ad un negozio e ad un museo, anche il ristorante della casa. Dal momento in cui è stato riprogettato da Philippe Starck esso offre una perfetta unione tra tradizione e modernità: Nella casa padronale del 1884 attendono l'ospite lampadari di cristallo posti in acquari, molto vetro ed argento nonché mobilio rettilineo e moderno.

Café de la Paix

Paris I France

www.cafedelapaix.fr
Interior Architecture: Pierre Yves Rochon (2003 renovations)
www.pyr-design.com
Photos: courtesy Café de la Paix

Since 1862, Café de la Paix is a real Paris institution—a classic that never gets out of style. Designed and realized by Alfred Armand, the café reminds guests of the splendor of the past till this day. Impressive frescos and stuccos, beautiful antiquities as well as precious furniture invite guests here to feel like the popular writer Émile Zola for a moment.

Das Café de la Paix ist eine echte Pariser Institution seit dem Jahr 1862 – ein Klassiker, der nie aus der Mode kommt. Entworfen und realisiert von Alfred Armand, erinnert das Café bis heute an den Glanz vergangener Tage. Beeindruckende Fresken und Stuckarbeiten, hübsche Antiquitäten sowie wertvolles Mobiliar laden hier dazu ein, sich einen Moment lang wie der berühmte Schriftsteller Émile Zola zu fühlen.

Depuis 1862, le Café de la Paix est une véritable institution parisienne – un classique qui n'a jamais cessé d'être à la mode. Conçu et réalisé par Alfred Armand, le café rappelle jusqu'à aujourd'hui les fastes du Second Empire. Des fresques impressionnantes et des stucs raffinés, de belles antiquités ainsi que des meubles précieux invitent à se sentir ici, un court instant, comme le célèbre écrivain, Émile Zola.

El Café de la Paix es una de las auténticas instituciones parisinas desde el año 1862 – un estilo clásico que nunca deja de estar de moda. Diseñado y realizado por Alfred Armand, el Café no deja de transmitir hasta nuestros días el Glamour de los tiempos pasados. Impresionantes pinturas al fresco y detalles estucados, preciosas antigüedades, así como el valioso mobiliario invitan a sentarse un rato, tal vez para sentirse durante algún momento como el famoso escritor Émile Zola.

Il Café de la Paix è una vera e propria istituzione di Parigi dall'anno 1862 – un classico che non è mai fuori moda. Progettato e realizzato da Alfred Armand, il Café mantiene ancora oggi lo splendore dei giorni passati. Impressionanti affreschi e stuccature, belle antichità nonché prezioso mobilio invitano in questo luogo a sentirsi per un momento come il famoso scrittore Émile Zola.

Le Saut du Loup

Paris I France

www.lesautduloup.com
Architecture: Philippe Boisselier
www.philippeboisselier.com
Photos: Joachim Frydman

Right in the heart of Paris in the Museum of Decorative Arts, with a beautiful view on the Tuileries, there is the Le Saut du Loup. This restaurant is characterized by its puristic, linear and minimal style and the black-and-white color provides an interesting contrast compared to the pompous environment. Light plays a very important role here—in the form of innovative ceiling lights and huge windows that give way to an amazing view to the Louvre and the Eiffel Tower.

Im Musée des Arts décoratifs, direkt an den Tuilerien, liegt mitten in Paris das Restaurant Le Saut du Loup. Mit seinem puristischen, linearen Stil des Minimalismus und der schwarz-weißen Farbgebung bietet es einen reizvollen Kontrast zur pompösen Umgebung. Dabei spielt Licht eine wichtige Rolle – in Form innovativer Deckenleuchten und der großen Fenster, die einen fantastischen Ausblick auf Louvre und Eiffelturm bieten.

Le restaurant Le Saut du Loup se trouve dans le Musée des Arts décoratifs, directement à côté des Tuileries, au beau milieu de Paris. Le style puriste, recourant aux lignes droites et au noir et blanc est du minimalisme le plus pur : il offre un contraste fascinant par rapport à un environnement architectural empreint de somptuosité. La lumière joue un rôle déterminant – sous la forme de luminaires innovants et de grandes fenêtres qui donnent une vue fantastique sur le Louvre et sur la Tour Eiffel.

En el Musée des Arts décoratifs, en el corazón de las Tullerías, en el centro de Paris, se ubica el restaurante Le Saut du Loup. Con su estilo purista y lineal tal y como lo impone el minimalismo y la coloración totalmente negra y blanca, se ha creado un contraste muy atractivo con el pomposo entorno. En el interior juega un papel muy importante la luz que queda asegurada con la ayuda de luminarias de techo de diseño innovador por una y unas enormes ventanas que por otra parte permiten que nos deleitemos con una vista fantástica sobre el Louvre y la Torre Eiffel.

Nel Musée des Arts décoratifs (Museo delle arti decorative), che si trova direttamente presso le Tuileries, a Parigi si trova il ristorante Le Saut du Loup. Con il suo stile puristico e lineare caratterizzato da minimalismo e da una colorazione bianco-nera, esso offre un attraente contrasto alla pomposità che lo circonda. In tutto questo la luce gioca un ruolo importante – sotto forma di lampade da soffitto innovative e di grandi finestre che offrono un fantastico panorama sul Louvre e sulla Torre Eiffel.

MĂ Restaurant

Berlin I Germany

www.ma-restaurants.de
Architecture: Anne Maria Jagdfeld
www.amjdesign.com
Photos: courtesy Adlon Holding GmbH

Those who visit a restaurant in the Hotel Adlon Kempinski Berlin might expect the exceptional—and will still be surprised by the subtle elegance of the MĂ. Inspired by the name MĂ, which is the Chinese word for horse, Anne Maria Jagdfeld created an ambience which is affected by exquisite materials such as cashmere, bronze and Wenge wood—with a huge, ancient clay horse form the Chinese Han dynasty watching over the restaurant.

Wer ein Restaurant im Hotel Adlon Kempinski Berlin besucht, erwartet vielleicht bereits das Außergewöhnliche – und wird dennoch von der feinsinnigen Eleganz des MĂ überrascht sein. Inspiriert vom Namen MĂ, dem chinesischen Wort für Pferd, entwarf Anne Maria Jagdfeld ein Ambiente, das geprägt ist von edlen Materialien wie Cashmere, Bronze und Wengeholz – bewacht von einem großen, jahrtausendealten Tonpferd aus der chinesischen Han-Dynastie.

Celui qui se décide pour un restaurant situé dans l'Hôtel Adlon Kempinski à Berlin s'attend, d'emblée, à quelque chose d'exceptionnel – et pourtant il ne manquera pas d'être surpris par l'élégance subtile du MĂ. Inspirée par le nom MĂ, le mot chinois pour cheval, Anne Maria Jagdfeld a créé une ambiance marquée par des matériaux nobles tels que le cachemire, le bronze et le bois de wengé – sous le regard d'un grand cheval d'argile de plusieurs milliers d'années sorti tout droit de la dynastie chinoise Han.

Aquél que visita un restaurante en el Hotel Adlon Kempinski de Berlín es muy posible que ya esté esperando encontrar lo nunca visto... pero aún así se quedará sorprendido por la refinada y exquisita, incluso ingeniosa elegancia, que encuentra en el MĂ. Inspirado por el nombre MĂ, la palabra china para el caballo, Anne Maria Jagdfeld diseñó un ambiente impregnado por los materiales nobles como el cachemira, el bronce y la madera de wengue custodiados todos ellos por el gran caballo de barro de miles de años de edad correspondiente a la dinastía Han.

Chi visita un ristorante nell'Hotel Adlon Kempinski di Berlino si attende forse già lo straordinario – e rimarrà tuttavia sorpreso dalla fine eleganza del MĂ. Ispirata dal nome MĂ, traduzione in cinese della parola cavallo, Anne Maria Jagdfeld ha progettato un ambientazione caratterizzata da materiali nobili quali cashmere, bronzo e legno wengé – sorvegliati da un grande cavallo di terracotta millenario proveniente dalla dinastia cinese Han.

Au Quai Restaurant

Hamburg I Germany

www.au-quai.com
Architecture: GMP Gerkan Marg & Partner
www.gmp-architekten.de
Photos: Gulliver Theis, courtesy Au Quai Restaurant

In summer, the most beautiful place of the Au Quai restaurant is definitely the panoramic terrace—with its fantastic view over the Hamburg harbor. However, this place has a lot more great views to offer for its guests behind the huge windows of the former refrigerating storage. What goes perfectly with it is the elegantly restrained interior which has been designed as an accomplished mixture of Nordic distinctiveness and Asian lightness.

Im Sommer ist der schönste Platz des Au Quai Restaurant ganz klar die Terrasse – mit dem groß-artigen Blick über den Hamburger Hafen. Doch auch hinter den großen Fensterfronten des ehema-ligen Kühlhauses bekommen die Gäste noch genug von der herrlichen Umgebung zu sehen. Dazu passt das vornehm zurückhaltende Interieur, das in einer gekonnten Mixtur aus nordischer Klarheit und asiatischer Leichtigkeit gestaltet ist.

En été, la plus belle place du restaurant Au Quai est bien sûr, la terrasse – elle donne un point de vue exceptionnel sur le port de Hambourg. Mais aussi derrière les vitrages de la façade de l'ancien entrepôt frigorifique, les visiteurs jouissent toujours d'une vue superbe. L'intérieur, d'une élégance discrète, associe avec beaucoup d'assurance la clarté nordique à la légèreté asiatique et s'harmonise à ce panorama privilégié.

El lugar más bonito en el restaurante Au Quai de Hamburgo es la terraza – obviamente, en verano. Desde aquí se goza de un maravilloso panorama del puerto de Hamburgo. Pero la verdad es que incluso detrás de los enormes ventanales de este antiguo almacén portuario refrigerado, les queda la suficiente vista a los comensales y, además, a tono con el interior, sumamente elegante, discreto y concebido con una mezcla muy elaborada entre el pragmatismo nórdico y la ligereza asiática.

In estate il posto più bello dell'Au Quai ristorante è naturalmente la terrazza – con il meraviglioso panorama sul porto di Amburgo. Tuttavia, anche dietro le grandi finestre dell'ex magazzino frigorifero gli ospiti hanno la possibilità di godersi molto bene una parte del meraviglioso panorama. A questo spirito si adattano gli interni raffinatamente discreti che rappresentano una riuscita miscela di chiarez-za nordeuropea e leggerezza asiatica.

Die Bank

Hamburg I Germany

www.diebank-brasserie.de
Architecture: SEHW Architekten
www.sehw.de
Photos: Carsten Brügmann

Eponym for Die Bank in Hamburg is the building in which this fine brasserie is located. Money has been the main business in the mortgage bank's former cash hall for more than 100 years. This past lives on at Die Bank, seeing the coined credit card numbers at the bar counter and the wine cellars thick former safe wall.

Namensgeber für Die Bank in Hamburg ist das Gebäude, in dem sich die feine Brasserie befindet. Über 100 Jahre lang wurde hier, in der ehemaligen Kassenhalle der Hypothekenbank, mit Geld gearbeitet. Bei den geprägten Kreditkartennummern am Bartresen und in der dicken früheren Tresorwand des Weinkellers lebt diese Vergangenheit im Restaurant Die Bank weiter.

Le nom pour Die Bank à Hambourg vient de l'immeuble où se trouve cette Brasserie élégante. Pendant plus de 100 ans, on a travaillé ici avec l'argent dans la salle des caisses de l'ancienne banque hypothé-caire. Ce passé se perpétue dans le restaurant Die Bank à travers les numéros de cartes de crédit im-primés sur le comptoir ainsi que dans le mur épais de l'ancien coffre-fort aujourd'hui utilisé comme cave à vins.

El origen del nombre para el restaurante Die Bank en Hamburgo es el edificio donde está ubicada esta finísima Brasserie, ya que durante más de 100 años aquí se encontraron las ventanillas del antiguo banco hipotecario y aquí se trabajaba con dinero contante y sonante. Esta tradición sigue viva en la actualidad en los números de tarjetas de crédito en la barra y el grueso muro de la antaño cámara acorazada que ahora hace de bodega.

Il nome Die Bank di Amburgo è stato dato da un edificio nel quale si trova una fine birreria. Per oltre cento anni, in questo luogo, nella ex sala sportelli della banca ipotecaria, si lavorava con soldi. Questo passato rivive nel ristorante Die Bank nei numeri di carta di credito impressi sul bancone del bar e nella spessa ex parete del tesoro della cantina del vino.

Sitzwohl Restaurant Bar

Innsbruck I Austria

www.restaurantsitzwohl.at
Architecture: Irmgrad Frank
www.irmgardfrank.at
Photos: courtesy Sitzwohl Restaurant Bar

When a chef sets a high value on fresh, ecologically correct ingredients, and wants to find exactly the same demand in her restaurant's design, Sitzwohl is the result. With her restaurant in Innsbruck, Irmgard Sitzwohl created a place that airs casual atmosphere with its warm colors, the many wooden elements and the fresh, lush apple-green on wall and seats. Still, Sitzwohl is well thought out, modern and very elegant at the same time.

Wenn eine Köchin Wert auf frische, ökologisch korrekte Zutaten legt, und genau diesen Anspruch auch im Design ihres Restaurants wiederfinden möchte, kommt dabei das Sitzwohl heraus. Irmgard Sitzwohl hat mit ihrem Innsbrucker Restaurant einen Ort geschaffen, der mit seinen warmen Farben, den vielen Holzelementen und dem frischen, satten Apfelgrün an Wänden und Sitzen Natürlichkeit ausstrahlt. Dabei wirkt das Sitzwohl gleichzeitig durchdacht, modern und sehr elegant.

Un restaurant tel que le Sitzwohl voit le jour quand une cuisinière accorde une importance toute particulière à des aliments frais et écologiquement corrects et désire retrouver exactement cette exigence dans le design de son restaurant. Irmgard Sitzwohl a créé dans son Restaurant à Innsbruck un lieu où rayonne le naturel : des couleurs chaudes, de nombreux éléments en bois et le vert pomme soutenu des murs et des chaises. Parallèlement, le Sitzwohl donne l'impression d'un design réfléchi, moderne et très élégant.

Cuando una cocinera centra sus exigencias en unos ingredientes frescos, ecológicos y adecuados y luego transmite este mismo requisito al diseño de su restaurante, se llega inequívocamente al Sitzwohl. Con su restaurante en Innsbruck, Irmgard Sitzwohl ha creado un lugar que con sus colores cálidos, el enorme número de elementos de madera y el color verde manzana, fresco y saturado, en las paredes y en los asientos, irradia pura naturaleza. Al mismo tiempo el Sitzwohl nos transmite el aspecto de muy meditado, moderno y elegante.

Se una cuoca dà valore a ingredienti freschi e rispettosi dell'ambiente, e vorrebbe ritrovare questa esigenza riprodotta nel design del proprio ristorante, il risultato di questa combinazione è senza dubbio il Sitzwohl. Irmgard Sitzwohl ha creato con il suo ristorante un luogo che con i suoi colori caldi, diversi elementi in legno e con il fresco e saturo verde mela di pareti e sedie irradia naturalezza. In questo il Sitzwohl è allo stesso tempo meditato, moderno ed estremamente elegante.

Hollmann Salon

Vienna I Austria

www.hollmann-salon.at
Architecture: Christian Prasser
www.cp-architektur.com
Photos: Christian Saupper, courtesy Hollmann Salon

Mundanely and contemporarily dining and celebrating in a dignified setting—this is what the Hollmann Salon in Vienna offers its guests. The modern and, at the same time, pristine restaurant is located in the Heiligenkreuzerhof and probably Vienna's oldest apartment building, owned by the Zisterzienser monastery of Heiligenkreuz. The overall picture of tradition and modern spirit creates a place to feel good and being pampered—on long tables or also in the cozy, open eat-in kitchen.

Mondän und zeitgemäß speisen und feiern in altehrwürdigen, heiligen Hallen – das bietet der Hollmann Salon in Wien. Das moderne und zugleich urige Restaurant hat seinen Sitz im Heiligen-kreuzerhof, dem vermutlich ältesten Zinshaus Wiens, im Besitz des Zisterzienserstifts Heiligenkreuz. Das Gesamtbild aus Tradition und Moderne ergibt einen Ort zum Wohlfühlen und Verwöhnen lassen – an langen Tafeln oder auch in der gemütlichen, offenen Wohnküche.

Prendre un repas festif dans un cadre à la fois mondain et actuel dans des halles vénérables – c'est ce que propose le Hollmann Salon à Vienne. Ce restaurant à la fois moderne et typique se trouve dans le Heiligenkreuzerhof, probablement l'immeuble le plus ancien de la ville, appartenant à la fondation des cisterciens de Heiligenkreuz. Cet ensemble, associant tradition et de modernité, créé un lieu de bien être où l'on peut jouir des plaisirs de la dégustation – à de longues tables ou encore dans une grande cuisine et salle à manger ouverte.

Comer, cenar y celebrar de forma mundana y conforme a los tiempos en un santuario sacrosanto y venerable, esto es lo que le ofrece el restaurante Hollmann Salon de Viena. Este restaurante tan moderno como rústico se encuentra ubicado en el Heiligenkreuzerhof, probablemente la casa arrendada más antigua de Viena y propiedad del convento cisterciense Heiligenkreuz. El cuadro conjunto de tradición y modernidad, ha creado un lugar para encontrase rotundamente bien y dejarse mimar – sentado en una larga mesa o bien en la confortable cocina comedor totalmente abierta.

Mangiare e festeggiare mondanamente e in uno spirito di contemporaneità in sale solenni e sacre – questo offre il Hollmann Salon di Vienna. Questo ristorante, moderno e allo stesso tempo rustico, si trova a Heiligenkreuzerhof, in quello che si ritiene essere l'edificio multipiano più antico di Vienna, di proprietà della fondazione cistercense Heiligenkreuz. La sintesi tra tradizione e modernità ha dato come risultato un luogo dove sentirsi bene e farsi viziare – nelle lunghe tavole o nella comoda e aperta cucina abitabile.

Haus Hiltl

Zurich | Switzerland

www.hiltl.ch
Architecture: Ushi Tamborriello
www.tamborriello.de
Photos: Felix Frey / www.blupics.com

Switzerland's first vegetarian restaurant has a tradition of more than a century—and new trends come from the Hiltl till this day. The interior of this recently renovated restaurant artfully ties in with old traditions: this is where stylish furniture and chandeliers meet innovative glass surfaces. And simple, modern stairs interestingly contrast the luxuriant antiquities.

Das erste vegetarische Restaurant der Schweiz gibt es bereits seit über 100 Jahren – und bis heute gehen vom Hiltl neue Trends aus. Das Interieur des frisch renovierten Restaurants knüpft mit modernen Elementen geschickt an alte Traditionen an: Hier treffen Stilmöbel und Kronleuchter auf innovativ gestaltete Glasflächen. Und eine schlichte, moderne Treppe bildet einen interessanten Kontrast zu üppigen Antiquitäten.

Le premier restaurant végétarien de Suisse existe déjà depuis plus de 100 ans – et le Hiltl n'a cessé jusqu'à ce jour de créer des tendances. L'intérieur du restaurant, récemment rénové, allie savamment des éléments modernes à d'anciennes traditions : ici des meubles de style et des lustres rencontrent des surfaces en verre innovantes. Un escalier moderne et sobre créé un contraste intéressant face à des antiquités aux formes opulentes.

El primer restaurante vegetariano de Suiza ya tiene una historia de más de 100 años... y desde entonces, hasta nuestros días, el Hiltl sigue marcando nuevas tendencias. En el interior de este recién renovado restaurante los elementos modernos enlazan hábilmente con las viejas tradiciones: aquí se emparejan los muebles de estilo y las arañas del techo con superficies innovadoras acristaladas. Unas escaleras modernas y sumamente simples contrastan de una forma muy interesante con las exuberantes y suntuosas antigüedades.

Il primo ristorante vegetariano aperto in Svizzera opera da più di cento anni – e fino ad oggi nascono a Hiltl nuove tendenze. Gli interni del ristorante da poco rinnovato si riallacciano abilmente a vecchie tradizioni grazie ad elementi moderni: Qui si incontrano mobili in stile e lampadari a corona su innovative superfici in vetro. Una scala sobria ed elegante rappresenta un elegante contrasto rispetto alle antichità esuberanti presenti in questo locale.

Grill-X

Casale Monferrato I Italy

Architecture: Romolo Stanco
www.romolostanco.com
Photos: Riccardo Cordera

Perspective is the basic idea of the architectural concept of Grill-X. Despite a very low budget and a construction time of just 13 days, architect Romolo Stanco managed to design a location and interior which have guests discover something new from every perspective. The dining tables are evocative of a Japanese sushi bar though—surrounded by the highly-modern ambience of flowing forms and clear color combinations.

Der Grundgedanke des architektonischen Konzepts von Grill-X liegt in der Perspektive. Trotz eines minimalen Budgets und gerade mal 13 Tagen Bauzeit ist es Architekt Romolo Stanco gelungen, einen Raum und eine Einrichtung zu schaffen, die die Gäste aus jedem Blickwinkel etwas Neues entdecken lassen. Die Reihe kleiner Essplätze erinnert dabei an eine japanische Sushibar – umgeben vom hochmodernen Ambiente fließender Formen und klarer Farbkombinationen.

L'idée centrale du concept architectural de Grill-X repose sur la perspective. En dépit d'un budget modeste, réduit à un minimum et d'un délai de construction de 13 jours seulement, Romolo Stanco, architecte a réussi à créer un espace et un aménagement grâce auquel les visiteurs ne cessent de découvrir quelque chose de nouveau. Une série de petites tables rappellent un bar japonais de Sushi – plongé dans une ambiance ultramoderne de formes fluides et des combinaisons de couleurs claires.

La idea básica del concepto arquitectónico para el Grill-X, sin lugar a dudas se centraba en la perspectiva. A pesar de disponer de un presupuesto mínimo y apenas 13 días de tiempo para la realización de la obra, el arquitecto Romolo Stanco ha logrado crear un espacio y un equipamiento en el que los invitados descubren algo nuevo cada vez que cambian su ángulo de vista. La fila de asientos pequeños recuerda un poco a un bar de Sushi japonés – rodeado de un ambiente sumamente moderno de formas fluidas y combinaciones de colores contundentes.

L'idea di base dell'impostazione architettonica del Grill-X sta nella prospettiva. Nonostante un budget minimo e quasi 13 giorni di lavori di costruzione, l'architetto Romolo Stanco è riuscito a creare uno spazio e un allestimento che fa scoprire agli ospiti qualcosa di nuovo ad ogni angolo di visuale. Le file di posti tavola ricordano un Sushi bar giapponese – circondato da elementi fortemente moderni caratterizzati da forme fluenti e da chiare combinazioni di colori.

ill bar...

of & *Vegetables grill bar...*

Acquadulza

Maccagno, Lago Maggiore I Italy

www.acquadulza.it
Architecture: Simone Micheli for SIST GROUP
www.simonemicheli.com
Photos: Jürgen Eheim

For the Acquadulza, designer Simone Micheli created an interior concept that generates a very own mood: one feels a bit like underwater—and far away from all earthly at the same time. The natural colors used in the Acquadulza are alienated by a special light concept, numerous glass and stainless steel surfaces appear futuristic, but still harmonize with the archaic stone walls and comfortable suites.

Designer Simone Micheli entwarf für das Acquadulza ein Interieurkonzept, das eine ganz eigene Stimmung erzeugt: Man fühlt sich ein bisschen wie unter Wasser – und zugleich weit weg von allem Irdischen. Natürliche Farben werden im Acquadulza durch ein besonderes Lichtkonzept entfremdet, zahlreiche Glas- und Edelstahlflächen wirken futuristisch, harmonieren aber mit den archaischen Steinmauern und bequemen Sitzgruppen.

Pour l' Acquadulza le designer Simone Micheli a mis au point un concept d'architecture intérieure qui crée une ambiance toute particulière : on a un peu l'impression d'être sous l'eau, et, en même temps, d'être très loin de ce qui est terrestre. Une conception de l'éclairage métamorphose les couleurs naturelles dans l'Acquadulza, de nombreuses surfaces de verre et d'acier prêtent à l'ensemble un aspect futuriste mais s'harmonisent toutefois aux murs de pierres archaïques et aux sièges confortables.

El diseñador Simone Micheli ideó para el Acquadulza un concepto de interiorismo que de una manera muy trabajada crea sensaciones muy propias, extrañas y hasta curiosas: el visitante se siente un poco como debajo del agua y al mismo tiempo enormemente lejos de todo lo mundano. Gracias a un concepto de iluminación muy especial, los colores naturales del Acquadulza se alinean, numerosas superficies acristaladas y de acero inoxidable proporcionan un aire futurista a la vez que armonizan perfectamente con los gruesos muros de piedra arcaicos y los confortables rincones creados.

Il progettista Simone Micheli ha ideato per l'Acquadulza un'impostazione di interni che genera una disposizione d'animo tutta particolare: Ci si sente un poco come sott'acqua – e contemporaneamente lontani da tutto ciò che è terreno. Presso l'Acquadulza i colori naturali vengono estraniati per mezzo di una particolare impostazione delle luci, diverse superfici in vetro e in acciaio danno un'impressione futuristica, ma sono in armonia con le arcaiche mura in pietra e i comodi gruppi tavolo.

1 Area Bar
2 Area Ristorante
3 Area servizi
4 Area wine butega

Plató Restaurant

Barcelona I Spain

Architecture: FFWD (Laia Guardiola Raventós & David Benito Cortázar)
www.ffwd.es
Photos: Robert Justamante Antolin

The moment of eating is a very special moment that is different time and again. The Plató Restaurant leaves this diversity its space: here, tables can be moved so that dining tables for one or two guests can be transformed into long tables for friendly get-togethers. Semi-transparent partition walls create privacy exactly where it is needed. And due to its direct contact to the street, the bar is a place of activity and communication.

Der Moment des Essens ist ein ganz besonderer Augenblick, der immer wieder anders ist. Das Plató Restaurant lässt dieser Vielfältigkeit ihren Raum: Hier können Tische verschoben werden, so dass aus Essplätzen für ein oder zwei Personen lange Tafeln für gesellige Gruppen werden. Semitransparente Trennwände schaffen genau dort Intimsphäre, wo sie gebraucht wird. Und die Bar ist durch ihren direkten Kontakt mit der Straße ein Ort der Aktivität und des Austauschs.

Le moment du repas est un instant tout particulier, toujours différent. Le Plató Restaurant ouvre un espace à une telle variété : le mobilier peut être déplacé si bien que des tables réservées à une ou deux personnes peuvent se transformer en tables festives pour des groupes conviviaux. Des séparations à demi transparentes créent une atmosphère intime là où elle est souhaitée. Et le bar, en raison de son contact direct avec la rue, s'impose comme lieu d'activités et d'échanges.

El momento de la comida es un acontecimiento cada vez distinto. El Plató Restaurant de Barcelona brinda el espacio necesario para esta pluralidad: aquí se pueden desplazar las mesas a gusto de los comensales y convertir las de una o dos personas en tablas largas para grupos enteros. Por medio de biombos semi transparentes se crean zonas de intimidad justo ahí donde se necesitan. En el bar del restaurante, gracias a su contacto directo con la calle, se ha conseguido un lugar de actividades y de intercambio.

Il momento del mangiare rappresenta un momento del tutto particolare, sempre diverso da un altro. Il Plató Restaurant da spazio a questa molteplicità: Qui i tavoli possono essere spostati, così che da posti a tavola per una o due persone si possono realizzare lunghe tavole per gruppi numerosi. Divisori semitrasparenti creano, laddove vengono utilizzati, una sfera intima. E il bar, grazie al suo contatto diretto con la strada, è un luogo di attività e di scambio.

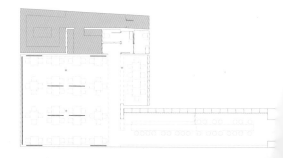

Negro de Anglona

Madrid I Spain

www.negrodeanglona.com
Architecture: Luis Galliussi
www.luisgalliussi.com
Photos: Luis Hevia, courtesy Negro de Anglona

The Negro de Anglona restaurant in Madrid is situated in the premises of the dignified Anglona palace. Architect Luis Galliussi and managing duo Juan & Borja Infante played with exactly this meaningful past when they arranged the interior. Reminiscences of the nobilities' great times are to be found everywhere—in pompous textiles, precious long white tables and, last but not least, in the illuminated pictures of European imperial palaces, which softly light up the restaurant's walls.

Das Restaurant Negro de Anglona in Madrid befindet sich in Räumen des ehrwürdigen Anglona-Palasts. Architekt Luis Galliussi und Managementduo Juan & Borja Infante spielten bei der Einrichtung mit genau dieser bedeutsamen Vergangenheit. Überall finden sich Reminiszenzen an die großen Zeiten des Adels wieder – bei pompösen Stoffen, edlen weißen Tafeln und nicht zuletzt bei den illuminierten Abbildungen europäischer Herrschaftspaläste, die die dunklen Wände des Lokals erhellen.

Le restaurant Negro de Anglona se trouve dans le bâtiment du vénérable palais Anglona. C'est justement ce passé glorieux que l'architecte Luis Galliussi et le duo de Managers Juan & Borja Infante déclinent de façon ludique pour l'aménagement intérieur. Partout, apparaissent des réminiscences du temps glorieux, – dans le choix des tissus somptueux, des services blancs et enfin dans l'éclairage : des cadres lumineux où sont représentés les palais des familles régnantes européennes illuminent les murs sombres du local.

El restaurante Negro de Anglona en Madrid se encuentra ubicado en los bajos de lo que fue una vez el Palacio del Príncipe de Anglona. Y justo este pasado significativo lo sacaron a relucir y resaltaron, tanto el prestigioso arquiteto Luis Galliussi, como el dúo de gerentes Juan & Borja Infante, a la hora de la concepción del restaurante. Por doquier nuestra vista se encuentra con reminiscencias que evocan los grandiosos tiempos de la nobleza e inspiraciones palaciegas, como telas pomposas, nobles mesas de blanco reluciente y, no en último lugar, las grandes ilustraciones iluminadas de palacios señoriales europeos que decoran las oscuras paredes del local.

Il ristorante Negro de Anglona di Madrid si trova negli ambienti del venerabile Palacio de Anglona. Nell'allestimento del ristorante l'architetto Luis Galliussie la coppia di dirigenti Juan & Borja Infante hanno giocato proprio con questo importante passato. Ovunque vi sono reminiscenze ai grandi tempi della nobiltà – pomposi tessuti, nobili tavole bianche e anche figure illuminate di palazzi signorili europei, che rischiarano le scure pareti del locale.

La Terraza del Casino

Madrid I Spain

www.casinodemadrid.es
Architecture: Jaime Hayon
www.hayonstudio.com
Photos: Nienke Klunder, courtesy Hayonstudio

The stylish, elegant La Terraza restaurant in the casino of Madrid presents itself in a new, spectacular look: modern unique pieces of design, combined with the restaurant's classical ambience, offer a one-of-a-kind and private atmosphere. Inventive cuisine creations give guests the good feeling that there is nothing left to be desired in this restaurant—and the creative, obliging interior style also emphasizes this idea.

Das stilvolle, elegante Restaurant La Terraza im Casino von Madrid, präsentiert sich im neuen, spektakulären Look: Moderne Designunikate ergeben zusammen mit dem klassischen Ambiente eine einzigartige und persönliche Atmosphäre. Die Gäste sollen hier durch einfallsreiche Küchenkreationen spüren, dass in diesem Restaurant alles für sie getan wird – und der kreative, verbindliche Einrichtungsstil unterstreicht diesen Gedanken ebenfalls.

La Terraza dans le Casino de Madrid, un restaurant élégant qui reflète au plus haut point un souci d'esthétique, se présente sous un Look nouveau et spectaculaire : des objets de design moderne uniques créent dans une ambiance toute classique une atmosphère originale et individualisée. Les visiteurs doivent sentir qu'ici tout est fait à leur intention, une volonté qui apparaît aussi bien dans les créations culinaires débordantes d'imagination que dans le style de l'aménagement créatif et accueillant.

El elegante restaurante La Terraza, ubicado en el Casino de Madrid, de estilo refinado, se presenta con un Look renovado y sumamente espectacular: modernas piezas de diseño únicas en combinación con el ambiente en lo restante clásico, crean una atmósfera única y personal. Por medio de creaciones culinarias de mucha fantasía aquí se quiere convencer a los invitados de que la casa hace todo lo que se puede para ellos. El estilo creativo y comprometido del interior también viene a subrayar esta percepción.

Il ristorante La Terraza del Casinò di Madrid, pieno di stile ed elegante, si presenta in un look nuovo e spettacolare: Moderni esemplari unici di progettazione creano, insieme ad un ambiente classico, un'atmosfera unica e personale. Grazie ad ingegnose creazioni di cucina, gli ospiti devono sentire che per loro in questo ristorante viene fatto di tutto – il creativo ed impegnativo stile di allestimento egualmente sottolinea questa idea.

Cubo

Ljubljana I Slovenia

www.cubo-ljubljana.com
Architecture: Katjusa Kranjc and Rok Kuhar Architects
www.raketa.si
Photos: Bogdan Zupan (page 129), Miran Kambic (pages 130-133)

The Cubo Restaurant in Ljubljana cleverly combines two rooms: the dark part with lots of fabric and the part with warm woods. Geometrical forms, which pick up the eponymous form of the cube, create a unit while gentle, harmoniously coordinated shades of brown provide for a homelike feeling in these architectonically linear rooms.

Das Restaurant Cubo in Ljubljana verbindet geschickt zwei Räume miteinander: Den dunkleren, mit Textilien gestalteten Bereich und den mit warmen Hölzern realisierten Teil des Lokals. Geometrische Formen, die die namensgebende Form des Kubus aufgreifen, schaffen eine Einheit, während sanfte, harmonisch aufeinander abgestimmte Brauntöne für ein heimeliges Gefühl in den architektonisch linearen Räumen sorgen.

Le restaurant Cubo à Ljubljana combine deux salles ingénieusement : une partie plus sombre décorée avec des étoffes et une partie plus chaude réalisée à partir de boiseries. Des formes géométriques déclinent la forme du cube qui donne son nom au local, créent une unité tandis qui des couleurs marron harmonisées les unes aux autres créent une atmosphère chaude dans les locaux d'une conception architecturale linéaire.

El restaurante Cubo en Ljubljana combina con habilidad dos estancias por su naturaleza muy distintas: la zona oscura realizada dominantemente con decoración de textiles y la parte del local realizada en tonos cálidos de madera. Formas geométricas que recogen la idea del cubo y nombre del local crean una unidad aparte, mientras una serie de tonos marrones, armónicamente coordinados entre sí, producen una sensación casera en las estancias arquitectónicamente lineales.

Il ristorante Cubo di Ljubljana unisce abilmente tra di loro due locali differenti: da una parte l'area dominata da un colore più scuro, caratterizzata da motivi tessili, dall'altra il settore del locale realizzato con legname chiaro. Le forme geometriche, che assumono una forma di cubo che dà il nome al locale, creano un'unità, mentre soffici tonalità di marrone intonate armonicamente l'una sull'altra generano una sensazione accogliente negli ambienti architettonicamente lineari.

Plato

Ljubljana I Slovenia

www.plato.si
Architecture: Katjusa Kranjc and Rok Kuhar Architects
www.raketa.si
Photos: Miran Kambic

A stylized wine cirrus is the central design element of the Plato café and restaurant in Ljubljana. Originating from the floor of the restaurant, this object cleaves its way through the room as a mural and partition to finally end as a wall decoration. This is where this vine provides hold to the room lighting. Dining becomes very pleasant on warmly colored suites, surrounded by gentle light.

Eine stilisierte Weinranke bildet das zentrale Designelement des Cafés & Restaurants Plato in Ljubljana. Das Objekt entspringt dem Fußboden des Lokals, setzt sich als Wandgestaltung und Raumteiler fort, um schließlich in einer Dekoration der Decke zu münden. Dort bietet das grafisch umgesetzte Klettergewächs der Raumbeleuchtung Halt. Im sanften Licht darunter lässt es sich auf Sitzgruppen in warmen Farbtönen angenehm speisen.

Des pampres de vigne stylisés fournissent l'élément central du design dans le Café & Restaurant Plato à Ljubljana. Jaillissant du plancher, ils déterminent la décoration murale, servent de motifs pour les meubles de séparation et aboutissent au plafond comme décoration. Là, cette végétation grimpante graphiquement stylisée tient l'éclairage du local. Au-dessous, à des tables individualisées, il est possible de prendre des repas dans une lumière douce et des couleurs chaudes.

Una cepa estilizada constituye el elemento de diseño central del Cafe Restaurante Plato en Ljubljana. La planta sale del suelo del local, continúa su camino como decoración de pared y partición de la estancia para finalmente terminar en la decoración del techo. Aquí, la planta trepadora realizada con medios gráficos detiene la iluminación del techo y consigue una suave luz que permite comer o cenar muy agradablemente sentado en pequeños grupos de asientos realizados en tonos cálidos.

Un viticcio stilizzato rappresenta l'elemento principale di design del caffè e ristorante Plato a Ljubljana. Tale elemento scaturisce dal pavimento del locale, prosegue quale caratterizzazione della parete e quale elemento divisorio del locale, per sfociare poi in una decorazione del soffitto. Sul soffitto, a questo rampicante, espresso graficamente, è fissata l'illuminazione. Esso trasmette una luce soffice in tonalità calde di colori sui gruppi tavolo e permette una piacevole consumazione del pasto.

Longtable Istanbul

Istanbul I Turkey

Architecture: GEOMiM – Muhmut Anlar
www.geomim.com
Photos: courtesy GEOMiM

Probably Istanbul's hippest restaurant, the Longtable, is situated—where else—in Nisantasi, the city's currently hottest district. And everybody who enters this place and strolls through the rooms on the catwalk, immediately senses that. Dark wood, finest leather and sparkling chandeliers cater to rich playboys to fell as comfortable as design fans who come here because of the attention-to-detail decoration.

Das vielleicht hippste Restaurant Istanbuls, das Longtable, befindet sich – wo sonst – in Nisantasi, dem derzeit angesagtesten Distrikt der Stadt. Das spürt auch sofort jeder, der das Lokal betritt und dort auf einem Catwalk durch die Räume flaniert. Dunkles Holz, feinstes Leder und glitzernde Kronleuchter sorgen dafür, dass sich hier wohlhabende Playboys genauso wohl fühlen wie Designfans, die wegen der detailverliebten Dekoration herkommen.

Le restaurant peut-être le plus en vogue d'Istanbul, le Longtable se trouve – ce qui ne saurait surprendre – dans Nisantasi, le quartier chic de la ville actuellement le plus à la mode. C'est ce que ressent immédiatement celui qui pénètre dans le restaurant et flâne dans les locaux comme sur un podium. Des bois sombres, des cuirs fins et des luminaires scintillants : ici les playboys fortunés se sentent aussi bien que des férus de design attirés ici par une décoration qui fascine par son attachement aux détails.

Es posible que sea el restaurante más en boga de toda Ístanbul – el Longtable – se encuentra en el barrio más de moda de la ciudad, en Nisantasi, ¿dónde si no? Lo percibe todo el mundo que entra en él y pasea por las habitaciones sobre el Catwalk puesto a tal efecto. Madera oscura, cuero fino, arañas de cristal y prismas resplandecientes se encargan de que los Playboys de talonario nutrido se encuentran igual de a gusto que los forofos por el diseño que vienen aquí a admirar la decoración enamorada del detalle.

Il Longtable, forse il ristorante più trendy di Istanbul, si trova – come potrebbe essere altrimenti – a Nisantasi, il distretto della città una volta più alla moda. Lo sente subito chiunque entri nel locale e passeggi tra i locali su una passerella. Legno scuro, finissimo cuoio, e lampadari a corona scintillanti fanno in modo che qui i playboy benestanti si sentano a proprio agio esattamente come le persone interessate al design, che vengono in questo ristorante a motivo delle decorazioni piene di dettagli.

Sushi Co

Istanbul I Turkey

www.sushico.com.tr
Architecture: Page Architecture and Design
www.page.com.tr
Photos: Louisa Nikolaidou

Those visiting the Sushi Co Restaurant in the district of Esentepe feel like in an Asian temple of the modern times—right in the center of Istanbul. Japanese decorated walls, wooden pillars from the Far East and a fine mosaic floor make guests feel as if they were not just in any sushi bar. Guests of the Sushi Co are dining sophisticatedly and good on precious massive wood floors—with a view of the sushi masters in the restaurant's open kitchen.

Wer das Sushi Co Restaurant im Stadtteil Esentepe betritt, fühlt sich wie in einem asiatischen Tempel der Neuzeit – mitten in Istanbul. In japanischem Stil dekorierte Wände, hölzerne Säulen aus dem Fernen Osten und ein feiner Mosaikboden geben den Gästen das Gefühl, hier nicht einfach in irgendeiner Sushibar zu sein. Auf edlen Massivholzböden speist man im Sushi Co anspruchsvoll und gut – mit Blick auf die Arbeit der Sushimeister in der offenen Küche.

Celui qui entre dans le restaurant Sushi Co situé dans le quartier de Esentepe à Istanbul a le sentiment de se trouver dans un temple asiatique des temps modernes – en plein centre d'Istanbul. Des murs portant une décoration de style japonais, des colonnes de bois venant de l'extrême orient et des sols de mosaïques raffinées donnent aux visiteurs l'impression de ne pas être dans un Sushibar quelconque. Dans le restaurant Sushi Co, on prend ainsi un bon repas sur un sol en bois massif – tout en observant le maître des Sushis dans une cuisine ouverte.

Aquél que entra en el restaurante Sushi Co en el barrio de Esentepe en seguida se siente como si se encontrase en un templo asiático de los tiempos modernos – en pleno centro de Ístanbul. Las paredes decoradas al estilo japonés, las columnas de madera traídas del lejano oriente y un impresionante suelo de mosaico, se encargan todos ellos de que los clientes en ningún momento se sientan como en un Sushibar de tres al cuarto. Sobre nobles suelos de madera maciza se come en el Sushi Co de forma exigente y de calidad – pudiendo ver al maestro cocinero de Sushi en su cocina abierta por todos los lados.

Chi mette piede nel ristorante Sushi Co, che si trova nel quartiere di Esentepe, si sente come in un tempio asiatico dell'era moderna – e ciò nel bel mezzo di Istanbul. Pareti decorate con motivi giapponesi, sale in legno ricche di motivi dell'Estremo Oriente, nonché un fine pavimento a mosaico danno agli ospiti la sensazione di non trovarsi un sushi bar qualsiasi. Sui nobili pavimenti in legno massiccio del Sushi Co si mangia in modo esigente e molto bene – con uno sguardo sul lavoro dello chef sushi nella cucina aperta.

Frame Bar

Athens I Greece

www.sgl-frame.gr
Architecture: Dimitrios Tsigos
www.tdc.gr
Photos: Dimitrios Tsigos

Everything's flowing in the Frame Bar in Athens—a table and chair do not only fit together in this bar—they are one. Shapes dynamically converge as by morphing, to harmoniously end as a whole. The result is a delicate space that inspires to enjoy new sensory experiences. Interesting material combinations invite guests haptically—and organic food and drinks let one's gustative nerves rejoice.

In der Frame Bar in Athen ist alles im Fluss – hier passen ein Tisch und ein Stuhl nicht einfach zusammen, sie sind eins. Formen, die wie durch Morphing ineinanderfließen, münden in ein harmonisches Ganzes. Es entsteht ein delikater Raum, der zu neuen Sinneserlebnissen inspiriert. Haptisch laden interessante Materialkombinationen dazu ein – und natürliche Speisen sowie Getränke lassen die Geschmacksnerven frohlocken.

Dans le Frame Bar à Athènes tout baigne dans un flux – ici les tables et les chaises ne s'accordent pas seulement entre elles, mais ne font qu'un. Des formes qui, animées par une métamorphose se mêlent et se fondent pour aboutir à une entité harmonieuse. C'est ainsi que se créé un espace délicat qui incite à de nouvelles expériences pour les sens. Des combinaisons de matériaux intéressantes invitent à des expériences tactiles – et des plats ainsi que des boissons naturelles réjouissent les papilles.

En el Frame Bar de Athen todo esta fluyendo: aquí una mesa y una silla no se corresponden simplemente, sino que son la misma cosa. Formas que se funden entre ellas, como si de un efecto de Morphing se tratase, desembocan en una integridad perfectamente armónica. Se crea un espacio delicado inspirando a nuevas sensaciones para los sentidos. Desde el sentido del tacto, interesantes combinaciones de materiales invitan a ello, y los alimentos naturales al igual que las bebidas, prometen un festín para el paladar.

Nel Frame Bar di Atene tutto è fluttuante – qui un tavolo e una sedia sono difficili da distinguere, in effetti sono una cosa sola. Forme che fluttuano le une nelle altre grazie al morphing, confluiscono in un tutto armonico. Ne deriva uno spazio delicato, che ispira la mente a nuove esperienze sensoriali. Dal punto di vista del tatto, interessanti combinazioni di materiale rendono l'atmosfera estremamente attraente, mentre e cibi e bevande naturali fanno gioire i nervi del gusto.

AMERICAS

STACK Restaurant & Bar

Las Vegas I USA

www.lightgroup.com
Architecture: GRAFT
www.graftlab.com
Photos: Ricardo Ridecos, courtesy GRAFT architects / MGM Mirage

Entering STACK Restaurant in Las Vegas is similar to a trip into an exciting and impressing canyon. Complex wooden panelings create a space that formally reminds one about the miracle of nature— and enhance it at the same time. A tailor-made light concept hereby emphasizes the different wall structures and thus guests are completely fascinated by the "Stack Canyons".

Das Restaurant STACK in Las Vegas zu betreten kommt einer Reise in einen aufregenden und beeindruckenden Canyon gleich. Aufwendige hölzerne Wandverkleidungen erschaffen einen Raum, der formal an ein Naturwunder erinnert – und dieses gleichzeitig weiterentwickelt. Ein maßgeschneidertes Beleuchtungskonzept betont dabei die unterschiedlichen Strukturen der Wände und zieht die Gäste so vollkommen in den Bann des „Stack-Canyons".

Pénétrer dans le restaurant STACK à Las Vegas ressemble à un voyage dans un Canyon fascinant et grandiose. Des revêtements muraux en bois raffinés créent un espace dont la forme évoque celle d'une merveille naturelle – une merveille naturelle dont l'évolution ne cesserait de se poursuivre. Une conception de l'éclairage sur mesure souligne les différentes structures des murs et entraîne les visiteurs dans le sillage du Stack-Canyon.

Entrar en el restaurante STACK de Las Vegas es parecido a realizar un viaje por un excitante e impresionante cañón. Laboriosos revestimientos de pared realizados en madera crean espacios que con su forma recuerdan a un milagro del mundo... y que al mismo tiempo lo sigue desarrollando. Un concepto de iluminación hecho a la medida viene a subrayar las diferentes estructuras de las paredes que, de esta manera, cautivan y hechizan a los visitantes ante los encantos del "Cañón Stack".

Entrare nel ristorante STACK di Las Vegas è simile ad un viaggio in un emozionante e impressionante canyon. Costosi rivestimenti in legno della parete creano uno spazio che nella forma ricorda un miracolo naturale – e contemporaneamente lo sviluppa ulteriormente. Un'impostazione di illuminazione fatta su misura sottolinea le differenti strutture delle pareti e attira ottimamente gli ospiti nell'incantesimo dei canyon posticci.

Blue Velvet Restaurant

Los Angeles I USA

www.bluevelvetrestaurant.com
Architecture: Tag Front
www.tagfront.com
Photos: Eric Axene

The open, elegant Blue Velvet Restaurant is situated right on top of the pool deck of the apartment building "The Flat". It includes the restaurant itself, a large terrace area at the pool as well as a roof garden which provides fresh fruits, vegetables and herbs for the kitchen. Lots of glass, a varied wall design, and lots of stone and abstract sculptures are characteristic here for a contemporary environment for successful downtowners.

Auf dem Pooldeck des Appartmenthauses „The Flat" befindet sich das offene, elegante Restaurant Blue Velvet. Es umfasst das Restaurant selbst, einen weiten Terrassenbereich am Pool sowie einen Dachgarten, der die Küche mit frischem Obst, Gemüse und Kräutern versorgt. Viel Glas, eine abwechslungsreiche Wandgestaltung, viel Stein und abstrakte Skulpturen sorgen hier für eine zeitgemäße Umgebung für erfolgreiche Downtowner.

Le restaurant Blue Velvet élégant et largement ouvert sur l'extérieur se trouve au niveau piscine de l'hôtel pour suites, studios et appartements « The Flat ». Il couvre un domaine qui englobe le restaurant, une large surface directement devant la piscine ainsi qu'un jardin terrasse qui alimente la cuisine en fruits, en légumes et en fines herbes. Beaucoup de verre, des décorations murales variées, des revêtements en pierres naturelles et de nombreuses sculptures abstraites constituent cet environnement contemporain très caractéristique pour une grande ville dynamique et gagnante.

El sumamente elegante y abierto restaurante Blue Velvet se encuentra en el Pooldeck del edificio de apartamentos "The Flat". Se trata tanto del restaurante en sí mismo, como en una amplia terraza alrededor de la piscina y un jardín que abastece el restaurante con fruta, verdura y hierbas frescas. Mucho cristal, una concepción muy variada de las paredes, mucha piedra y esculturas abstractas, materializan el ambiente actual y a tono con los Yuppies del Downtown Los Angeles.

Al pool deck del residence "The Flat" si trova il Blue Velvet, un ristorante aperto ed elegante. Esso comprende il ristorante vero e proprio, un'ulteriore area di terrazze presso la piscina nonché un orto coperto che fornisce la cucina di frutta fresca, verdura e piante aromatiche. Molto vetro, pareti variegate, molta pietra e sculture astratte rappresentano un ambiente moderno per persone di successo che vengono dal centro cittadino.

BG Restaurant

New York City I USA

www.bergdorfgoodman.com
Architecture: Kelly Wearstler
www.kellywearstler.com
Photos: courtesy Bergdorf Goodman

Those who are looking for something special for their shopping break in New York are perfectly right in the BG Restaurant of Bergdorf Goodman. Apart from coffee and cakes, this sophisticated restaurant also offers delicious tea menus in a comfortable, stylish atmosphere. With hand-painted wallpapers, deep armchairs from the 18th century and soft blue and grey shades on the walls, guests should feel cozy and comfortable just like as if it was a private visit.

Wer sich für seine Shoppingpause in New York etwas Besonderes wünscht, der ist im BG Restaurant von Bergdorf Goodman genau richtig. Das schicke Tagesrestaurant bietet neben Kaffee und Kuchen auch leckere Tea Menüs in einer angenehm durchgestylten Atmosphäre. Mit handbemalten Tapeten, tiefen Sesseln aus dem 18. Jahrhundert und zarten Blau- und Grautönen an den Wänden sollen sich die Gäste so wohl fühlen wie bei einem ganz privaten Besuch.

Celui qui fait du shoping à New York et qui, entre deux magasins, désire vivre quelque chose de particulier, ne saurait manquer de visiter le BG Restaurant de Bergdorf Goodman. Ce restaurant de jour chic, offre, indépendamment du café et des gâteaux, de bons menus « tea » dans une atmosphère agréable et de bon goût. Les tapisseries peintes à main, les fauteuils profonds du 18ème siècle, les bleus et les gris tendres des murs invitent les visiteurs à se sentir aussi bien que dans un espace privé découvert à l'occasion d'une visite.

Todo aquél que para un pequeño descanso en una ajetreada mañana de Shopping en Nueva York busca algo muy especial, lo tiene en el BG Restaurant de Bergdorf Goodman. Aparte de una buena taza de café y pastelitos, el elegante restaurante de día ofrece deliciosos menús de Tea en un ambiente muy agradable y con mucho estilo. Con sus papeles pintados a mano en las paredes, espaciosos sillones del siglo 18 y las delicadas tonalidades en azul y gris en las paredes, el decorador ha perseguido que los clientes se encuentren tan a gusto como en una visita muy particular.

Chi desidera in New York qualcosa di particolare per la pausa shopping, ha trovato nel BG Restaurant di Bergdorf Goodman il suo posto ideale. Questo ristorante diurno alla moda offre, oltre a caffè e a torte, anche ghiotti menu a base di tè in un'atmosfera caratterizzata per intero dallo stile. Con tappezzerie dipinte a mano, poltrone profonde del diciottesimo secolo e tenere tonalità bluastre e grigiastre sulle pareti, gli ospiti si devono sentire a loro agio come nel corso di una visita privata.

GILT

New York City I USA

www.giltnewyork.com
Architecture: Patrick Jouin
www.patrickjouin.com
Photos: Michael Kleinberg

The French designer Patrick Jouin did not impose a completely new concept on the GILT Restaurant in New York—he just arranged new elements which emphasize the room's unique late 19th century flair. The gilt walls and cathedral-like ceilings are now complemented by airy, light suites, heavy lounge furniture for comfortable rests as well as by graphical elements that are framing the bar area.

Der französische Designer Patrick Jouin stülpte dem Restaurant GILT in New York kein völlig neues Konzept über – er arrangierte einfach neue Elemente, die das einzigartige Flair der Räume aus dem späten 19. Jahrhundert unterstreichen. Die vergoldeten Wände und kathedralenartigen Decken werden nun ergänzt durch leichte, helle Sitzgruppen, schwere Loungemöbel zum gemütlichen Ausruhen sowie durch grafische Elemente, die den Barbereich gestalten.

Le designer français Patrick Jouin n'a pas imposé au restaurant GILT à New York une conception entièrement nouvelle – il a seulement introduit de nouveaux éléments qui soulignent le charme original de ces locaux de la fin du 19ième siècle. Les murs dorés et les plafonds genre cathédrale sont complétés par des groupes des sièges clairs et légers, mais aussi par des sièges profonds de salon qui incitent à une repos agréable. Des éléments graphiques d'une structure marquante définissent l'espace du bar.

Lo que no hizo el diseñador francés Patrick Jouin con el restaurante GILT en Nueva York es encasquetarle un nuevo concepto como si de un sombrero nuevo se tratase... lo único que hizo fue disponer una serie de elementos nuevos para subrayar el aire único en su género que se respira en el interior de las estancias que datan de los finales del siglo XIX: ahora, las paredes doradas y los techos a modo de catedral medievo, se ven complementados por grupos de asientos de color claro, pesados muebles de máximo confort para el relax total, así como una serie de elementos gráficos que forman la zona de la barra.

Il progettista francese Patrick Jouin non ha dato al ristorante GILT di New York un'impostazione totalmente nuova – egli ha semplicemente arrangiato nuovi elementi che accentuano l'atmosfera unica degli ambienti del tardo diciannovesimo secolo. Le pareti dorate e soffitti quasi da cattedrale vengono ora completati da gruppi tavolo leggeri e chiari, pesanti mobili da salotto per un comodo riposo nonché elementi grafici che caratterizzano l'area attrezzata a bar.

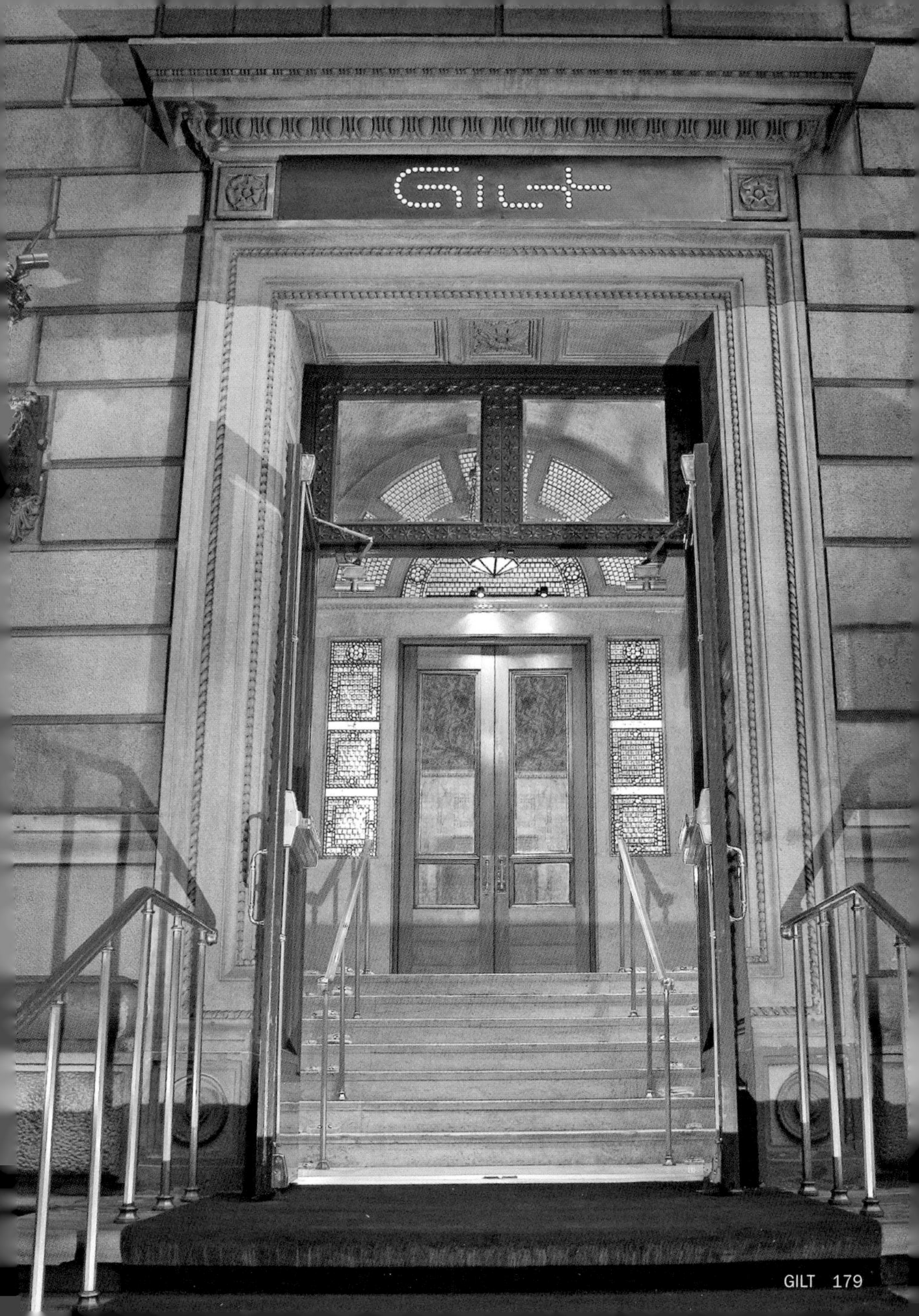
GILT

Peach House

San Gabriel, CA I USA

www.peachhouseyogurt.com
Architecture: Make Architecture
www.makearch.com
Photos: John Edward Linden

The Peach House in San Gabriel is the world's first café which committed itself to an innovative summer dish: the frozen yoghurt. The restaurant's interior thereby reflects the typical characteristics of this light refreshment. White walls symbolize the yoghurt that shows frozen in all its layers. Fruity yellow and orange shades remind someone of juicy peach sauces and the rounded off shapes have guests think of flowing milk.

Das Peach House in San Gabriel ist das erste Café, das sich einer innovativen Sommerspeise verschrieben hat: dem Frozen Yoghurt. Das Interieur des Lokals spiegelt dabei die typischen Eigenschaften der leichten Erfrischung wider. Weiße Wände symbolisieren den Joghurt, der sich gefroren in Schichten auffächert. Fruchtige Gelb- und Orangetöne erinnern an saftige Pfirsichsoßen. Und die abgerundeten Formen lassen die Gäste an fließende Milch denken.

Le Peach House à San Gabriel est le premier café qui se soit voué à une spécialité estivale innovante : le Frozen Yogurt. L'intérieur du local reflète les propriétés typiques de ce léger rafraîchissement. Des murs blancs symbolisent le yaourt qui se déploie en couches une fois glacé. Des tons jaunes et orange rappellent les sirops de pêche intenses. Et les formes arrondies incitent le visiteur à penser à des flots de lait.

La casa de los melocotones o Peach House en inglés en San Gabriel es el primer Café que ha puesto todas sus cartas en un alimento de verano sumamente innovador, el Frozen Yoghurt o yogurt congelado. Hasta el interior del local refleja las características típicas de un ligero refresco: las paredes blancas simbolizan el yogurt cuyas capas congeladas se abren a modo de abanico, los frutosos tonos amarillos y naranja recuerdan jugosas salsas de melocotón, y las formas redondeadas consiguen que más de uno de los visitantes piense en leche en movimiento.

Il Peach House di San Gabriel è il primo caffè che si è totalmente dedicato ad un innovativo piatto estivo: lo yogurt ghiacciato. Gli interni del locale rispecchiano le tipiche caratteristiche del leggero rinfresco. Le pareti bianche rappresentano lo yogurt gelato a strati. Tonalità giallastre e arancio ricordano gustose salse alla pesca. Le forme arrotondate fanno pensare a latte fluente.

Forneria

Rio de Janeiro I Brazil

Architecture: Isay Weinfeld
www.isayweinfeld.com
Photos: Leonardo Finotti

The philosophy of the Forneria restaurant in Rio is: "understatement". One large room has a consciously puristic effect with its long, open kitchen unit. There is a series of small tables made of warm wood on the plain floor and framed movie posters serve as a decoration. The long kitchen block strikes the eye due to its conveniently natural wood paneling. And the simple wood-concrete look even continues outside on the restaurant's terrace.

Das Motto des Restaurant Forneria in Rio lautet: „Understatement". Ein weiter Raum wirkt mit seiner langen, offenen Küchenzeile bewusst puristisch. Auf dem nüchternen Boden stehen eine Reihe kleiner Tische aus warmem Holz, gerahmte Filmposter dienen als Dekoration. Der lange Küchenblock fällt durch seine angenehm natürliche Holzverkleidung ins Auge. Und auf der Terrasse setzt sich der schlichte Holz-Beton-Look fort.

La devise du restaurant Forneria à Rio est de créer un ensemble d'une esthétique qui s'impose tout en renonçant aux effets spectaculaires. Une grande pièce associée à une longue cuisine intégrée est d'un effet volontairement puriste. Sur un sol nu se trouve une rangée de petites tables en bois chaud ; d'anciens affiches de cinéma encadrées servent de décoration. La cuisine en forme de bloc allongé frappe par le naturel agréable de son revêtement en bois. Et sur la terrasse du restaurant le look sobre du bois et du béton continue à se déployer.

El lema del restaurante Forneria de Río es lo que los ingleses llaman el "Understatement" o el "que no sea nada aparente". La amplia estancia con su larga cocina abierta en uno de los lados nos brinda un buscado estilo purista. En el suelo frío se alinea una hilera de pequeñas mesas de una madera de tono muy cálido, pósteres de películas enmarcados forman la decoración a lo largo de la pared. El alargado bloque de cocina destaca por su revestimiento de Madera confortablemente natural. Como continuación, este mismo Look desnudo de madera y hormigón se vuelve a encontrar en la terraza.

Il Motto del ristorante Forneria di Rio è: "Understatement". Un ampia sala con il suo blocco cucina lungo e aperto dà un'impressione coscientemente puristica. Sul sobrio pavimento si trova una serie di piccoli tavoli in legno caldo, mentre poster incorniciati riportanti immagini tratte da film servono quale decorazione. Il lungo blocco cucina salta all'occhio con il suo rivestimento in legno naturale. E sulla terrazza prosegue il disadorno look legno-calcestruzzo.

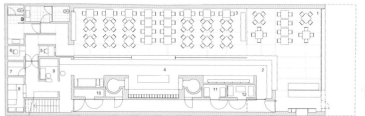

FORNERIA

Fasano

São Paulo I Brazil

www.fasano.com.br
Architecture: Isay Weinfeld
www.isayweinfeld.com
Photos: Gavin Jackson

Embedded into the exclusive hotel of the same name, the Fasano is the most-awarded restaurant of the Brazil metropolis São Paulo. The Fasano offers international dishes with an Italian touch in an ambience that leaves nothing to desire: fine materials, dark, chocolate-colored wood and tasteful panellings create a room climate which is as casual as demanding.

Das meistprämierte Restaurant der brasilianischen Metropole São Paulo ist das Fasano – eingebettet in das exklusive, gleichnamige Hotel. Das Fasano offeriert internationale Speisen, die italienisch geprägt sind. In einem Ambiente, das keine Wünsche offen lässt: Edle Stoffe, dunkles, schokoladenfarbenes Holz und geschmackvolle Wandverkleidungen schaffen ein ebenso legeres wie anspruchsvolles Raumklima.

Le restaurant le plus souvent récompensé de la métropole brésilienne São Paulo est le Fasano – intégré dans l'hôtel exclusif du même nom. Le Fasano offre des mets internationaux marqués surtout par la cuisine italienne. L'ambiance comble tous les voeux : des étoffes opulentes, des bois sombres évoquant le chocolat ainsi que des décorations murales du meilleur goût créent un espace empreint certes de légèreté mais à la hauteur de toutes les exigences.

El restaurante de la metrópolis brasileña de São Paulo que más premios ha cosechado es el Fasano – incrustado en el exclusivo Hotel del mismo nombre. El Fasano ofrece platos internacionales ligeramente italianizados, y lo hace en un ambiente que no deja ningún sueño por realizar: nobles telas, madera oscura cual chocolate y revestimientos de pared de un gusto exquisito y refinado, crean todos ellos un clima especial que discute entre el ligero y el exigente.

Il ristorante più premiato della metropoli brasiliana San Paolo è il Fasano – inserito nell'ambito dell'hotel esclusivo che porta lo stesso nome. Il Fasano offre piatti internazionali con caratterizzazione italiana. E' un ambiente che non lascia deluso alcun desiderio: Tessuti nobili, legno scuro di color cioccolato e rivestimenti di parete pieni di gusto creano un ambiente interno leggero ed allo stesso tempo esigente.

ASIA/ AUSTRALIA

Gingerboy

Melbourne I Australia

www.gingerboy.com.au
Architecture:Elenberg Fraser
www.e-f.com.au
Photos: Dianna Snape

Gingerboy takes a popular Asian tradition to Melbourne—the tradition of street markets and hawkers. A luminous advertising therefore leads the way to the restaurant entrance from the street already. Large windows grant insights into the Asian inspired interior with its large lantern installation and the bamboo covered walls.

Gingerboy holt eine beliebte asiatische Tradition nach Melbourne – die der Straßenmärkte und fliegenden Händler. Deshalb weist bereits von der Straße eine grelle Leuchtreklame zum Eingang des Restaurants. Große Fensterflächen gewähren Einblicke in das asiatisch inspirierte Interieur mit seiner großen Laterneninstallation und den bambusverkleideten Wänden.

Gingerboy fait vivre à Melbourne une tradition asiatique populaire – celle des marchés de rue et des marchants ambulants. C'est pourquoi une réclame lumineuse signale dans la rue l'entrée du restaurant. Des fenêtres généreuses laissent apparaître un intérieur inspiré par l'Asie que rappelle de grandes installations de lanternes et des murs recouverts de bambous.

El Gingerboy nos trae una de las muy queridas tradiciones asiáticas a la ciudad de Melbourne – la de los mercados callejeros y los comerciantes errantes. De ahí que un reclamo chillón de neón encima de la entrada del restaurante llama la atención desde la misma calle. Amplias superficies de grandes ventanales invitan a admirar el interior inspirado en la misma Asia con sus grandes instalaciones de lámparas colgantes y sus paredes revestidas de bambú.

Il Gingerboy porta a Melbourne una tradizione asiatica di successo, quella dei mercati di strada e dei mercatini volanti. Per questo motivo, una pubblicità luminosa annuncia già dalla strada l'ingresso al ristorante. Grandi finestre permettono uno sguardo negli interni ispirati da motivi asiatici, con il grande impianto della lanterna e le pareti rivestite di bambù.

Vue de Monde

Melbourne I Australia

www.vuedemonde.com.au
Architecture: Elenberg Fraser
www.e-f.com.au
Photos: Dianna Snape

Finest French cuisine in the center of Melbourne? Welcome to the Vue de Monde restaurant! Here, the members of design studio Elenberg Fraser made it their business to emphasize the chef's high demand—and give reason to smile at the same time. A mirror on the ceiling therefore provides the opportunity to watch the chef closely while preparing the food. And opulent curtains as well as preciously set tables are contrasting with simple illumination concepts and loosely hanging cables.

Feinste französische Küche mitten in Melbourne? Willkommen im Vue de Monde Restaurant! Das Designstudio Elenberg Fraser machte es sich hier zur Aufgabe, den hohen Anspruch des Küchenchefs zu unterstreichen – und gleichzeitig Anlass zum Schmunzeln zu geben. So bietet ein Deckenspiegel die Möglichkeit, den Küchenchef ganz genau zu beobachten. Und opulente Vorhänge sowie edel gedeckte Tische kontrastieren mit simplen Beleuchtungsideen und offen hängenden Kabeln.

La cuisine française la plus raffinée au centre de Melbourne ? Bienvenue au restaurant Vue de Monde ! Le studio de design Elenberg Fraser s'est donné pour tâche de mettre en scène les exigences élevées du chef de cuisine – et en même temps de donner l'occasion de sourire. C'est ainsi qu'un miroir de plafond donne la possibilité d'observer très exactement le maître de cuisine. Et des rideaux opulents ainsi que des tables richement couvertes créent un contraste ironique avec une conception de l'éclairage volontairement sans façon où des câbles pendent librement.

¿Cocina francesa de primera en pleno corazón de Melbourne? ¡Bienvenidos al restaurante Vue de Monde! En este caso, el estudio de diseñadores Elenberg Fraser tenía el cometido de subrayar las elevadas exigencias del Chef, al mismo tiempo que dar motivo a alguna que otra sonrisa. De ahí que un espejo hábilmente colocado en el techo brinda la oportunidad de observar al Chef durante su trabajo. Por otra parte, las opulentas cortinas así como las mesas puestas a la perfección, contrastan con las ideas de iluminación sumamente simplistas y los cables que cuelgan.

Finissima cucina francese a Melbourne? Benvenuti nel ristorante Vue de Monde! Lo studio di progettazione Elenberg Fraser si è fissato lo scopo di sottolineare l'elevato standard voluto dal chef della cucina – e contemporaneamente dare adito ad un sorriso di compiacimento. Lo specchio posto sul soffitto offre la possibilità di osservare con attenzione lo chef della cucina. Inoltre, opulenti tende e tavoli ricoperti finemente contrastano con le semplici idee di illuminazione e i cavi pendenti visibili.

Le Lan

Beijing I China

Architecture: Philippe Starck
www.philippe-starck.com
Photos: Patricia Bailer

A spacious, surreal appearing restaurant that plays with the guests' fantasy and provides space for individualism at the same time—this is the challenge, Philippe Starck brilliantly coped with in the Le Lan in Beijing. Apart from opulent dining rooms and lounges, the restaurant's theatrical interior also provides individual booths, which are hiding behind massive curtains and thus allow for an untroubled dinner with good friends in a tent-like atmosphere.

Ein weitläufiges, surreal wirkendes Restaurant, das mit der Fantasie der Gäste spielt und zugleich Raum für Individualität bietet – diese Herausforderung hat Philippe Starck im Le Lan in Beijing bravourös gemeistert. Das theatralische Interieur des Restaurants bietet neben opulenten Speisesälen und Lounges auch individuelle Separees, die sich hinter wuchtigen Vorhängen verstecken und so in einer zeltartigen Atmosphäre ein ungestörtes Dinner mit guten Freunden ermöglichen.

Ce vaste restaurant, à l'effet surréel, joue avec l'imagination des visiteurs et offre en même temps un espace à l'individualité – c'est un tel défi que Philippe Starck a su maîtriser avec brio dans Le Lan à Pékin. L'intérieur du restaurant, théâtral, offre aussi, à côté de salles à manger opulentes et de Lounges, des salons particuliers dissimulés derrière d'imposants rideaux qui permettent de dîner avec des amis sans être dérangé dans une atmosphère analogue à celle d'une tente.

Un restaurante de grandes espacios con aspecto surrealista que juega con la fantasía de los comensales y al mismo tiempo ofrece espacio para el individualismo: este reto Philippe Starck lo ha superado con éxito y con nota en el restaurante Le Lan de Beijing. Aparte de salas de comer de tamaño generoso y Lounges, el interior teatral del restaurante ofrece apartados individuales que se esconden detrás de enormes cortinas para permitir una comida o cena ininterrumpida rodeada de buenos amigos en un ambiente que nos recuerda mucho a una jaima árabe.

Un ristorante ampio, dall'atmosfera surreale, il quale gioca con la fantasia degli ospiti e contemporaneamente offre spazio per l'individualità – realizzando gli interni del Le Lan Philippe Starck ha vinto, ed in modo superbo, questa sfida. Gli interni teatrali del ristorante offrono accanto ad opulente sale da pranzo e saloni anche ambienti separati individuali che si nascondono dietro tende imponenti, ed in questo modo permettono di creare una cena senza disturbo con buoni amici in un'atmosfera quasi da tenda.

Blue Frog

Mumbai I India

www.bluefrog.co.in
Architecture: Serie Architects
www.serie.co.uk
Photos: Fram Petit

Bar, restaurant and live music performance club in the same place—the Blue Frog is the most versatile of all restaurants in Mumbai. The interior, designed by the international design office Serie, combines these different facets: the circular suites nestle up against the center stage. The suites are gently inclining so that guests can enjoy excellent views on the live acts even from the backmost seats.

Bar, Restaurant und Livemusikklub in einem – das Blue Frog ist das Vielseitigste unter den Restaurants in Mumbai. Das Interieur, gestaltet vom internationalen Designbüro Serie, vereint genau diese unterschiedlichen Facetten: Wie einzelne Zellen schmiegen sich die kreisrunden Sitzgruppen rund um die Centerstage. Dabei steigen sie in ihrer Höhe an, sodass die Gäste auch von den hintersten Plätzen noch einen hervorragenden Blick auf die Liveacts haben.

Rassemblant à la fois un bar, un restaurant et un club de musique – le Blue Frog offre le restaurant le plus varié à Mumbai. L'intérieur conçu par le bureau de design international Serie réunit exactement ces différentes facettes : telles des cellules les groupes de sièges ronds se regroupent autour du « Centerstage ». Ils sont placés en gradin si bien que les hôtes se trouvant aux dernières places ont encore une très bonne vue sur les « Liveacts ».

Bar, restaurante, sala de espectáculos para música en vivo, todo en uno – el Blue Frog es el más multifacético entre todos los restaurantes de Mumbai. El interior realizado por los diseñadores internacionales Serie reúne precisamente estas facetas tan distintas: como si fueran celdas, las mesas perfectamente redondas con sus sillas redondean el escenario principal al tiempo que se elevan en altura para permitir que hasta los comensales de las mesas más traseras tengan una perfecta vista sobre el espectáculo.

Bar, ristorante e club di musica dal vivo in una cosa sola – il Blue Frog è, tra i ristoranti di Mumbai, quello più variegato. Gli interni, progettati dallo studio di design internazionale Serie, uniscono in modo preciso o queste diverse caratteristiche: i gruppi tavolo circolari si appoggiano attorno al centro del palco come singole celle. Essi si sviluppano in altezza, così che anche gli ospiti dei posti più posteriori possono avere un ottima visuale su ciò che avviene dal vivo sul palco.

Nooch Express

Singapore I Singapore

Architecture: Karim Rashid
www.karimrashid.com
Photos: CI&A Photography

The Nooch Express is a noodle bar—the Asian version of a fast food restaurant. Planned by design guru Karim Rashid, this restaurant, however, conveys it as anything else but the usual fast food pabulum: shocking pink and lush lime green meet soft, curved forms. And the exterior walls are decorated with a dazzling mosaic, penetrated by softly rounded windows which grant extraordinary insights.

Das Nooch Express ist eine Noodle-Bar – die asiatische Variante eines Fast-Food-Restaurants. Durchgestylt von Designguru Karim Rashid vermittelt es aber alles andere als den üblichen Fast-Food-Einheitsbrei: Knalliges Pink und saftiges Limegreen treffen hier auf weiche, runde Formen. Und die Außenwände sind mit schillerndem Mosaik verziert, durchbrochen von sanft gerundeten Fenstern, die außergewöhnliche Einblicke gewähren.

Le Nooch Express est un Noodle-Bar – la variante asiatique d'un restaurant Fast-Food. Conçu par le gourou du Design Karim Rashid, il donne une toute autre impression que celle qu'engendre l'uniformité habituelle des restaurants rapides : des roses vifs, des verts limettes juteux sont juxtaposés à des formes douces et rondes. Et les murs extérieurs sont décorés de mosaïques aux couleurs vives, interrompus par des fenêtres dont les arrondis s'ouvrent sur des perspectives inhabituelles.

El Nooch Express es un Bar especializado en pasta – la variante asiática de los restaurantes de comida rápida. Su diseño vanguardista viene de la mano del Gurú de diseño Karim Rashid y hace todo lo contrario del "Café para todos" que se esperaría de un establecimiento de estas características: un rosa más que chillón combinado con un verde lima no menos alarmante chocan aquí con formas suaves totalmente redondeadas. Las paredes del exterior se han decorado con un mosaico reluciente opalizante con aperturas suavemente redondeadas a modo de ventana que permiten una visión excepcional del interior.

Il Nooch Express è un Noodle-Bar – la variante asiatica di un ristorante fast food. I suoi interni sono stati realizzati dal guru dello stile Karim Rashid; tuttavia il Nooch Express trasmette tutto fuorché la miscela di elementi tipica dei ristoranti fast food: rosa vivace ed un succoso verde lime qui si incontrano con forme soffici e circolari. Le pareti esterne sono ornate di un cangiante mosaico, interrotto da finestre sofficemente tondeggianti, che permettono visioni straordinarie.

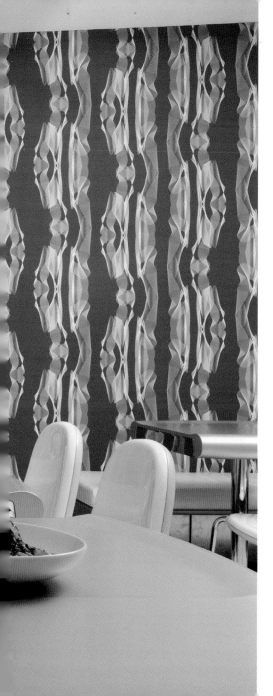

INDEX

Acquadulza
Lungolago Girardi
21010 Maccagno (Va)
Italy
www.acquadulza.it

Au Quai Restaurant
Große Elbstr. 145b-d
22767 Hamburg
Germany
www.au-quai.com

Baccarat
11, place des Etats-Unis
75116 Paris
France
www.baccarat.fr

BG Restaurant
5th Avenue at 58th Street
New York, NY 10019
USA
www.bergdorfgoodman.com

Blue Frog
Mathuradas Mills Compound
NM Joshi Marg, Lower Parel
Mumbai, 400013
India
www.bluefrog.co.in

Blue Velvet Restaurant
750 Garland Ave
Los Angeles, CA 90017
USA
www.bluevelvetrestaurant.com

Café de la Paix
5, Place de l'Opéra
75009 Paris
France
www.cafedelapaix.fr

Cubo
Smartinska c. 55
1000 Ljubljana
Slovenia
www.cubo-ljubljana.com

Die Bank
Hohe Bleichen 17
20354 Hamburg
Germany
www.diebank-brasserie.de

Eetbar Dit
Snellestraat 24-26
5211 's-Hertogenbosch
The Netherlands
www.eetbar-dit.nl

Fasano
Rua Vittorio Fasano 88
São Paulo
Brazil
www.fasano.com.br

Forneria
Rua Aníbal de Mendonça, 112
Ipanema
Rio de Janeiro
Brazil

Frame Bar
Deinokratous 1
Athens Kolonaki 10675
Greece
www.sgl-frame.gr

GILT at The New York Palace Hotel
455 Madison Avenue
New York, NY 10022
USA
www.giltnewyork.com

Gingerboy
27–29 Crossley Street
Melbourne, VIC 3000
Australia
www.gingerboy.com.au

Grill-X
Via Madre Teresa di Calcutta 1
Casale Monferrato
Italy
www.spiedonny.com

Haus Hiltl
Sihlstrasse 28
8001 Zürich
Switzerland
www.hiltl.ch

Hollmann Salon
Grashofgase 3/Heiligenkreuzerhof
1010 Vienna
Austria
www.hollmann-salon.at

Kungsholmen
Norr Mälarstrand, Quay 464
11220 Stockholm
Sweden
www.kungsholmen.com

La Terraza del Casino
Calle de Alcalá 15
28014 Madrid
Spain
www.casinodemadrid.es

Le Lan
4/F Twintowers B-12
Jianguowenmai Avenue
Chaoyang District, Beijing
China

Le Saut du Loup
107, Rue de Rivoli
75001 Paris
France
www.lesautduloup.com

Longtable Istanbul
Tesvikiye Street No:45/A
34367 Nisantasi/Istanbul
Turkey

MĂ Restaurant
Behrenstraße 72
10117 Berlin
Germany
www.ma-restaurants.de

Mathias Dahlgren
S. Blasieholmshamnen 6
10327 Stockholm
Sweden
www.mathiasdahlgren.com

Negro de Anglona
Calle de Segovia 13
28005 Madrid
Spain
www.negrodeanglona.com

Nooch Express
501 Orchard Road
Wheelock Place 02-16
Singapore

Olivomare
10 Lower Belgrave Street
London SW1W 0LJ
UK
www.olivolondon.com

Peach House
531 W Valley Blvd
San Gabriel, CA 91776
USA
www.peachhouseyogurt.com

Plato
Ajdovscina 1
1000 Ljubljana
Slovenia
www.plato.si

Plató Restaurant
Gran Vía Corts Catalanes 408
08015 Barcelona
Spain

Praq Restaurant
Darthuizerberg 69
3825 BL Amersfoort
The Netherlands
www.praq.nl

Sake No Hana
23 St James's Street
London SW1A 1HA
UK
www.sakenohana.com

Sitzwohl Restaurant Bar
Stadtforum/Gilmstraße 4
6020 Innsbruck
Austria
www.restaurantsitzwohl.at

STACK Restaurant & Bar
Mirage Resort & Casino
3400 S. Las Vegas Blvd
Las Vegas, NV 89109
USA
www.lightgroup.com

Sushi Co
Buyukdere Street
Astoria Towers No:127
34394 Esentepe/Istanbul
Turkey
www.sushico.com.tr

Vue de Monde
430 Little Collins Street
Melbourne, VIC 3000
Australia
www.vuedemonde.com.au

Wahaca
66 Chandos Place
London WC2N 4HG
UK
www.wahaca.co.uk

Other titles by teNeues

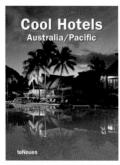

ISBN 978-3-8327-9309-8

ISBN 978-3-8327-9274-9

ISBN 978-3-8327-9237-4

ISBN 978-3-8327-9247-3

ISBN 978-3-8327-9234-3

ISBN 978-3-8327-9308-1

ISBN 978-3-8327-9243-5

ISBN 978-3-8327-9230-5

ISBN 978-3-8327-9248-0

Size: **15 x 19 cm**, 6 x 7½ in., 224 pp., **Flexicover**, c. 200 color photographs,
Text: English / German / French / Spanish / Italian
www.teneues.com

Other titles by teNeues

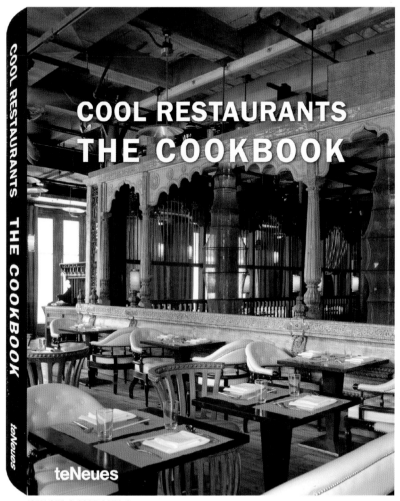

ISBN 978-3-8327-9271-8

Size: **23.5 x 29.5 cm**, 9¼ x 11¾ in., 144 pp., **Hardcover with jacket**,
129 color photographs, Text: English / German
www.teneues.com

teNeues' new Cool Guide series

ISBN 978-3-8327-9293-0

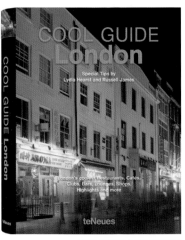

ISBN 978-3-8327-9294-7

ISBN 978-3-8327-9295-4

ISBN 978-3-8327-9296-1

Size: **15 x 19 cm**, 6 x 7 ½ in., 224 pp., **Flexicover**, c. 250 color photographs,
Text: English / German / French / Spanish

www.teneues.com